From

· · · · · · · · · • • • • • • • • • • • • • • • · · · · · · · · ·

To

· · · · · · · · · • • • • • • • • • • • • • • • · · · · · · · · ·

Date

· · · · · · · · · • • • • • • • • • • • • • • • · · · · · · · · ·

YOUNG AND FOUND

YOUNG AND FOUND

A 40-DAY DEVOTIONAL FOR YOUNG ADULTS AND TEENS

JOSEPH OLA

ANU OLA

Word Alive

PREFACE

Consider the following headlines:

- Young People Are 'Lost Generation' Who Can No Longer Fix Gadgets, Warns Professor — *The Telegraph*[1]
- Dear Millennials — A Letter To The Lost Generation — *Medium*[2]
- A Lost Generation — *Church Times*[3]
- Millennials Are the New Lost Generation — *The Atlantic*[4]

Wherever you turn in the world today—within and without the church—there seems to be a plague of *lostness* associated with young people. Arguably so, some are lost in the sense that they are far from knowing and/or accepting their true identity. Some are lost in the sense of being aimless (or aiming for too many things and hitting at none). Many of us seem not to know what to live for or die for. Suicide and depression are at an all-time high among millennials.[5]

Recent surveys have found that, unlike the older generation, young adults and teens have a more bleak chance at identifying with any religiosity.[6] We now live in a dispensation where pre-40 adults are less likely than adults age 40 and above to reckon religion as being 'very important' in their lives—and this is not a reality exclusive to the western world, it is also the reality of 'countries that are less affluent and more religious, such as Iran, Poland and Nigeria.'[7]

In 2019, Barna Group conducted a global research on millennials. There were more than 15,000 young adults ages 18 to 35 from 25 countries across all the continents who participated in the research. They were asked about their goals, fears, relationships, routines and beliefs in order to uncover a number of key trends. One of the key findings of that research was this:

> only 1 in 3 millennials feel that someone believes in them while the remaining two

thirds desperately crave to be believed in, too.[8]

The implication is clear: to secure the future involves believing in the younger generation. As they search for identity and trade their childhood dependence for adult autonomy, young people need the church to give them a genuine sense of belonging. This will happen when older believers begin to make themselves available to journey alongside these young people, modelling for them a desirable picture of who they can be.

This kind of leadership will look like *mentorship* and *reverse mentorship*. Gone are the days when discipleship was all about following a few lessons from a syllabus designed according to some systematic theology. Young people want Christian models and mentors—people that can relate with their fast-changing world and model for them how to live out their faith in this context of rapid dynamism (mentorship). However, they also want leaders who are willing to learn from their youthful perspectives to life and religion, too (reverse mentorship). They do not want a leader that has an answer for every question—Google does that for them—rather they will thrive in relating with a Christian leader whose job isn't to have all the definitive answers but to help create a hunger in them to chase their questions into Christ's loving arms.

This is the drive and motive that birthed *Alive Mentorship Group (AMG)* and consequently, this devotional series. In 2015, out of a desperate desire to disciple a few teenagers within our sphere of influence at the time, we decided to create a platform on social media—the second home of these digital natives—where we could create a community of sincere learners doing life together. We decided that we are going to be open and transparent with these young folks about our successes and failures—turning them into conversation starters (whether as blog-type posts or vlogs). Looking back 5 years later, that group of few teenagers had become a community of thousands of teenagers and young adults . . . to the glory of God.

In those 5 years, we have witnessed interesting testimonies of transformation among these young folks just as much as we have been transformed ourselves. (Some of them generously shared a bit about that in the blurb beginning on the next page.) The daily reflections in this devotional had been curated from some of the earliest posts on AMG. We've titled the collection *Young and Found* as our attempt to change the narrative. Being *young* does not have to mean being *lost.* The overall testimony of AMG is that of a family of millennials who are young, yes, but they are *young and found* in Christ. May that be your testimony, too.

Joseph and Anu Ola
September 2020

WHAT MEMBERS OF ALIVE MENTORSHIP GROUP ARE SAYING

I joined AMG after I came across the testimony of the wedding of Pastor & Mrs Ola from a viral Facebook post titled *'I Married You'*. I was endeared to the simplicity they showcased and how they both made Jesus known through their wedding. (This, they continue to do now through their marriage.) Since joining AMG, however, I have gained more than I bargained for. I have gained godly wisdom for living, godly mentorship, dear friends in Pastor Kola and ma Eleos. My faith has been stirred and encouraged in so many ways through the faith-lifting lessons they share. Hugely, AMG has taught me to learn lessons from my everyday experiences and be open to share them when necessary. I've gained a family in AMG for which I will always be grateful.
— **Annabelle** | *London, UK*

Joining AMG gave me an insight and understanding into God's love for me through different teachings. One experience that remains forever etched in my heart is the **#50HappyPeople** challenge. We were encouraged to practice random acts of kindness towards all manner of people over a period of time. I have always been a giver—howbeit at my convenience and discretion. That experience, however, has since lived with me and shaped many events in my life. Thank you for all you do, Pastor Kola and Sister Eleos. Your light shines brighter, always!
— **Teniola** | *Atlanta GA, United States*

There is something unique about AMG—how Pastor Joseph and his wife journalise their daily activities through the lens of God's Word. The daily posts have always been inspiring and a source of spiritual growth for myself and everyone I share the posts with.
— **Abiodun** | *Lagos, Nigeria*

I didn't know Pastor Kola and Mrs Ola well when I joined AMG but I had read their story and somehow I felt like I needed to be connected to them even from afar. It's just funny how the stories they are not ashamed to share tend to fit my context and bless me. My major takeaway since I joined AMG is **intentionality**. The story of how they *intentionally* maintained communication in their long-distance relationship blessed me and taught me intentionality in relating with my friends and family. I keep learning from the AMG community everyday!
— **Adepeju** | *Abeokuta, Nigeria*

Knowing Pastor Kola since 2011 in Gombe State has been a blessing in my life. I joined AMG to know more about the journey of faith and to be spiritually nourished on a daily basis. Besides, their love story which they always share generously has helped me in my marriage as well. God bless you Pastor Kolawole and Eleos.
— **Evangelist Damilola** | *Pretoria, South Africa*

AMG has been an amazing family to me. I joined as a young person looking for mentorship, growth, friendship and support. I found all that and more! Now I help build this marvellous Christian family. The books, posts, daily talks and interactions bless thousands of lives every day and I pray these continue.
— **Ayodeji** | *Lisbon, Portugal*

Joining AMG has been a great light for us—learning and hearing different views from great minds. Pastor Ola and Mrs Eleos share so passionately in a way that resonates very well with young people. Besides, the teams they have set up work efficiently together to ensure that we are growing spiritually and physically. We are grateful to be part of such a great family.
— **Ifeoluwa** | *Liverpool, UK &*
Israel | *Lagos, Nigeria.*

AMG has been a blessing to me. Since I joined, it has been from one level of growth to another. AMG taught me how to read books — something I thought I couldn't do. Pastor Ola taught me how to be sincere with God even with the ugly details of my life. His wife, God bless her, taught me that the Holy Spirit can be your friend. The Olas model Christ to me from a platform of honesty, sincerity and simplicity. It's such a great privilege that I got to know them and be a part of the AMG family.
— **Osama** | *Calabar, Nigeria*

I like to think of AMG as one beautiful family of God. I joined AMG with the purpose of learning more about God and how to navigate life purposefully as a youth in this age and time. At the time, I struggled with maintaining a personal time with God but the transformation I've experienced from the *#YesterdayDaily* posts, monthly book reviews and the mind blowing contributions from other group members have been beyond words. These have helped shape me for the better. JKO and Eleos are a blessing to this generation. I celebrate you both!
— **Racheal** | *Oklahoma City, United States*

AMG has indeed been a mentorship and learning platform which has tremendously blessed me. Pastor Joseph writes so well that whenever I read any of his posts, I'm ministered to in a special way. I will always be grateful to God for the day I joined AMG.
— **Esther** | *Nigeria*

I joined AMG to improve my spiritual life in a community of young adults with like minds studying God's Word. It has been an awesome, life-changing experience ever since I joined. I thank God for the leadership of this great movement and for being a part of it. To God be the glory.
— **John** | *UK*

I'm delighted at the success story of AMG thus far. I say this because I am privileged to be a member of the platform right from its inception. I do not take for granted the direct access we all have to Joseph and Eleos. I love you both! Thanks for the privilege to serve with you. I give this devotional a 10/10 rating and do recommend it for everyone out there. I am persuaded of one message you cannot but get from this book—the 4 words that everyone on AMG readily relates with: "YOU ARE NOT ALONE." Happy Reading!
— **Peter Bright** | *Lagos, Nigeria*

My cousin introduced me to AMG when I relocated to the UK because I couldn't find a youth group where practical issues relatable to young Christians are being discussed. As a young Christian, I knew I needed a daily reminder of the Christian life and how to live it out without getting caught in the motions. AMG provides this and I feel grateful and always look forward to learn daily as I grow.
— **Blessing** | *UK*

AMG has been a blessing to me. I have always loved the simplicity of Pastor Kolawole Ola and his wonderful wife. This showed in every write-up we read on the platform. I am fascinated by how life-transforming truths are being shared in a very simple but powerful way through these write-ups and videos. I am happy to be a part of the AMG family!
— **Tobiloba** | *Aachen, Germany*

I joined AMG at a young age and I got a very good opportunity to learn so much from the daily posts by Pastor Ola. It got even better with the 'book reading' feature added later on. I'm glad I got this opportunity.
— **Busola** | *Ondo State, Nigeria*

I once said to Pastor Joseph, *"When I grow up, I want to be like you!"* Both himself and his wife have been a blessing to all of us on AMG.

— **Ritah** | *Gulu, Uganda*

AMG has been a tremendous help to me because the context of the posts are always relatable and I really appreciate the honesty with which the posts are written because it makes you feel like you are not alone in your struggles or mistakes. Besides, you also learn how to approach the same situation differently and get better results.

— **Iyanuoluwa** | *Plymouth, UK*

BOOKS BY THE AUTHORS*

Books by Joseph and Anu

1. *Young and Found*
2. *Marriage in View*
3. *Bumpy But Sweet (A Love Story)*

Books by Joseph

1. *Pandemic Joy: Making Sense of Life's Uncertainties*
2. *Is This Opportunity From God?: 7 Checkpoints for Discerning Divine Opportunities*
3. *#Unaddicted: Finding Freedom from Sex-related Addictions*
4. *Waiting Compass: Finding God when He seems to delay*
5. *Alive: Living in the Power of Grace and Truth*
6. *The Salvation Journey*

*Details about these titles are available on the last few pages of this book

CONTENTS

Acknowledgments	xxvii
1. Building Competence *by Joseph Ola*	1
2. Pay Attention To Your Life *by Anu Ola*	5
3. "God Told Me..." Seriously? *by Joseph Ola*	9
4. Assume the Best *by Joseph Ola*	13
5. S-O-A-P It *by Joseph Ola*	17
6. Time-Out *by Joseph Ola*	21
7. Configured for Tomorrow *by Anu Ola*	25
8. Casual Sex? *by Joseph Ola*	29
9. Premarital Sex *by Joseph Ola*	33
10. I Can Do Bad All by Myself *by Joseph Ola*	37
11. #NOSUM *by Joseph Ola*	41
12. Honour Your Parents *by Anu Ola*	45
13. Attitude Is Everything *by Joseph Ola*	49
14. From Fear To Faith (1) *by Joseph Ola*	53
15. From Fear To Faith (2) *by Joseph Ola*	57

16.	Justified Cheating? *by Joseph Ola*	61
17.	Mutual Submission *by Anu Ola*	65
18.	Enjoy Life *by Joseph Ola*	69
19.	We Are All Teachers *by Joseph Ola*	73
20.	There's an "Angel" in You! *by Joseph Ola*	77
21.	Honour God's Servants *by Joseph Ola*	81
22.	Submission in Marriage *by Anu Ola*	85
23.	We All Have Issues *by Joseph Ola*	89
24.	Your Weakness Is Not the Issue *by Joseph Ola*	93
25.	You Never Know *by Joseph Ola*	97
26.	Secret Prayers *by Joseph Ola*	101
27.	Kill Your Hate *by Anu Ola*	105
28.	The Other Side of Wisdom *by Joseph Ola*	109
29.	Looking for Some Magic? *by Joseph Ola*	113
30.	Godly Money Management (1) *by Joseph Ola*	117
31.	Godly Money Management (2) *by Joseph Ola*	121
32.	Godly Money Management (3) *by Joseph Ola*	125
33.	Godly Money Management (4) *by Joseph Ola*	129
34.	How To Journey Into the Unknown (1) *by Joseph Ola*	133

35. How To Journey Into the Unknown (2) *by Joseph Ola*	137
36. How To Journey Into the Unknown (3) *by Joseph Ola*	141
37. Tell It! *by Anu Ola*	145
38. lastminute.com (1) *by Joseph Ola*	149
39. lastminute.com (2) *by Joseph Ola*	153
40. lastminute.com (3) *by Joseph Ola*	157
Notes	161
Index	165
About the Authors	167
About the Book	169

Copyright © 2020 Joseph and Anu Ola
All rights reserved.
ISBN: 9798692071453

Word Alive, UK
www.josephkolawole.org

Bible Versions used:
Amplified Bible (AMP) Copyright © 2015 by The Lockman Foundation, La Habra, CA 90631. All rights reserved.; **Contemporary English Version (CEV)** Copyright © 1995 by American Bible Society; **Easy-to-Read Version (ERV)** Copyright © 2006 by Bible League International; **English Standard Version (ESV)** The Holy Bible, English Standard Version. ESV® Text Edition: 2016. Copyright © 2001 by Crossway Bibles, a publishing ministry of Good News Publishers.; **GOD'S WORD Translation (GW)** Copyright © 1995 by God's Word to the Nations. Used by permission of God's Word Mission Society.; **Good News Translation (GNT)** Copyright © 1992 by American Bible Society; **International Children's Bible (ICB)** The Holy Bible, International Children's Bible® Copyright© 1986, 1988, 1999, 2015 by Tommy Nelson™, a division of Thomas Nelson. Used by permission.; **J.B. Phillips New Testament (PHILLIPS)** The New Testament in Modern English by J.B Phillips copyright © 1960, 1972 J. B. Phillips. Administered by The Archbishops' Council of the Church of England. Used by Permission.; **Jubilee Bible 2000 (JUB)** Copyright © 2000, 2001, 2010 by Life Sentence Publishing, Inc.; **King James Version (KJV)** Public Domain; **Living Bible (TLB)** The Living Bible copyright © 1971 by Tyndale House Foundation. Used by permission of Tyndale House Publishers Inc., Carol Stream, Illinois 60188. All rights reserved.; **The Message (MSG)** Copyright © 1993, 2002, 2018 by Eugene H. Peterson; **New Century**

Version (NCV) The Holy Bible, New Century Version®. Copyright © 2005 by Thomas Nelson, Inc.; **New International Reader's Version (NIRV)** Copyright © 1995, 1996, 1998, 2014 by Biblica, Inc.®. Used by permission. All rights reserved worldwide.; **New International Version (NIV)** Holy Bible, New International Version®, NIV® Copyright ©1973, 1978, 1984, 2011 by Biblica, Inc.® Used by permission. All rights reserved worldwide.; **New King James Version (NKJV)** Scripture taken from the New King James Version®. Copyright © 1982 by Thomas Nelson. Used by permission. All rights reserved.; **New Life Version (NLV)** Copyright © 1969, 2003 by Barbour Publishing, Inc.; **The Passion Translation (TPT)** The Passion Translation®. Copyright © 2017 by BroadStreet Publishing® Group, LLC. Used by permission. All rights reserved. thePassionTranslation.com; **Worldwide English (New Testament) (WE)** © 1969, 1971, 1996, 1998 by SOON Educational Publications; **Tree of Life Version (TLV)** Tree of Life (TLV) Translation of the Bible. Copyright © 2015 by The Messianic Jewish Family Bible Society.

*To the members of **Alive Mentorship Group**.*
Thanks for allowing us to pour into you.

ACKNOWLEDGMENTS

We will like to appreciate the **members of Alive Mentorship Group** for the priceless privilege of learning together across the multiple social media platforms where we converge. It's amazing to watch a WhatsApp group of 12 teenagers grow into a global family of thousands of teenagers and young adults within 5 years. As much as you gave us the access to pour into you what we are learning as we journey through life, we are also grateful for your priceless contributions in the AMG family and for the precious lessons we have learnt from many of you. The questions you've asked us often become learning points for us before they become learning points for you. We will always be grateful for the gift of you all.

Specific shout out to the AMG Team working tirelessly behind the scene to make the community engaging, well-resourced and secure: **Adepeju Disu, Osama Osarenkhoe, Busola Badejo, Ayodeji Daramola, Paul Ilori, Peter Bright, Esther Adesegun and Bolanle Adewumi.** God bless you all.

We will also like to thank **John Hulse** and every member of the Life Group he led while I (Joseph) was in Bradford between 2015 and 2016. It was the series of conversations we had and the challenge we gave ourselves on journalling that taught me (and my wife by proxy) how to journal and share unreservedly from our life's experiences with the members of AMG.

We will also like to extend our gratitude to the **countless Angels** packaged in human flesh whom God had sent our way in our mentoring journey — these are simply too many people to begin to name them one by one. Massive thanks to the leaders and members of our church family, The Apostolic Church, Liverpool; the *Missio Africanus* Leadership Team under the servant leadership of Dr Harvey Kwiyani; our spiritual parents and mentors — Prof and Prof (Mrs) Fatusi, Pastor John and Deaconess Margaret Ameobi, Pastor (Mrs) Alby Oduneye, Pastor and Deaconess Davies, Dr Joseph Olowe,

Pastors Peter and Bukola Adewole and Reverend Olusola and Reverend (Mrs) Oyenike Areogun.

Most significantly, we thank the Chief Shepherd of our souls. How good is it to be able to say that even though we are *young*, we are *found* in Him!

1

BUILDING COMPETENCE
BY JOSEPH OLA

*"That the man of God may be competent,
equipped for every good work."
(2 Timothy 3:17 ESV)*

One of my memorable conversations with my mentor happened on the corridor outside his office sometime in 2010. I had watched him juggle so many responsibilities brilliantly—both on the home front, his career in academia and his church responsibilities. I had questions and he had a few minutes, so we met each other halfway. *"How are you able to combine so many things effortlessly?"* I asked. With a smile and without batting an eye, he gave me a three-point response:

Competence, Character and the Grace of God.

What does competence look like? I believe it looks like knowing the things you are good at and majoring on those—and always seeking to be better at them. There is nothing that trumps productivity like dissipating our energies on too many things. It's okay to not be an all-rounder. To be competent in some things means to be incompetent in some other things—and that's absolutely alright.

Ever since I embraced this principle, it has made a difference in my life. With time, I discovered the beauty of relationships. God created us with a bent towards somethings and a bent away from other things. As such, your competence makes up for someone else's incompetence and vice-versa.

Over to you . . .

- *What are you really good at?*
- *How do you plan to get better at it?*
- *Is there a skill you are lacking which makes you feel inadequate? How should you respond in light of the fact that "it's okay to not be an all-rounder"?*

2

PAY ATTENTION TO YOUR LIFE
BY ANU OLA

*"The man said to me, "Son of man, **look carefully** and **listen closely** and **pay attention** to everything I am going to show you, for that is why you have been brought here.*
Tell the people of Israel everything you see."
(Ezekiel 40:4 NIV)

Imagine that you are placed before an ongoing construction in the centre of your city and an Angel tells you to make sure you *observe everything* the construction workers are doing. Each line. Each cubit. Each measure is of great importance... If you knew the reason for such observation, I am sure you may be willing to try it out. But what if you were not shown the bigger picture and simply told to go each day to the construction site, take notes and observe. Would *not knowing* put you off?

Possibly.

Our lives are like that. We are all like a construction site—a work in progress—and God is concerned with every inch of it. Each empty room. Each broken pot. The chipped tables. The unmade beds. The overgrown lawn. The beautiful family portrait. The salty soup, sloppy kitchen—every nook in our lives is of great importance and significance to Him. And they are all bundles of lessons. Each gap between our afflictions; each resentment and honour—they are all tailored to bring us to where we should be. So the issues you have gone through and the ones you are going through now deserve strict observance. As such, when you overcome them, you will be able to see the lessons therein and share it with your *Israel*.

> *All praise to the God and Father of our Master, Jesus the Messiah! Father of all mercy! God of all healing counsel! He comes alongside us when we go through hard times, and before you know it, he brings us alongside someone else who is going through hard times so that we can be there for that person just as God was there for us.*

— 2 Corinthians 1:3-4 MSG

Over to you . . .

- *What will it look like to start paying attention to your life? (Tip: Start keeping a daily journal reflecting on the lessons you are learning from your daily experiences—successes and failures alike.)*
- *Is there someone in your life right now whom God has brought alongside you to encourage with a lesson you have learnt in the past?*

TODAY'S PRAYER

Thank You God for creating me in Your image and orchestrating every detail of my life. I receive the grace to be a careful observer of all that you are doing in me, for me and through me that I may be better equipped to be a blessing to others in Jesus' name. Amen.

Young & Found   JOSEPH OLA | ANU OLA

3
"GOD TOLD ME..." SERIOUSLY?
BY JOSEPH OLA

"...I was worshiping, when suddenly I heard a loud voice behind me, a voice that sounded like a trumpet blast"
(Revelations 1:10 TLB)

The first time I took notice of the beautiful lady I married, it happened in a moment of worship. I had just finished leading a Bible Study at a Youth Camp in Northern Nigeria and was worshipping God in appreciation for the grace He supplied in facilitating the Bible Study with clarity when I felt like He stopped me in my tracks and said to me *"look behind you to the bookstand."* I stopped. I looked. Yes there was a bookstand with books displayed for sale on it. And yes! — there was a beautiful lady standing by the table checking the books out! The rest of the story, well, is still being written...

Once upon a time, I cringe when I hear some Christians say things like *"God said to me..."* or *"God told me..."* When I hear such audacious claims, my mind wonders, *"Where did the conversation take place?"* However, as I grew in my walk with God, I started 'hearing God' myself. And in my experience, I feel more open to receive whatever He wants to say to me when I'm in a moment of worship. As soon as my mind is shifted from earthly distractions and focused on engaging the *invisible* in praise and adoration, my *inner ears and eyes* get opened and accessing God becomes possible.

Bottomline: Don't let anything choke off your worship moments. Find time to make worshiping God a regular thingy. And who knows, you might find yourself looking back in worship one of these days and find, well, some blessing that will last you for the rest of your life!

"God Told Me..." Seriously? | 11

Over to you . . .

- *All of our lives should be lived in light of worshipping God. What will it look like to start being intentional as a worshipper every single day? (Tip: Keep a daily discipline of spending time alone with God — some people call this 'Quiet Time'.)*
- *Do you struggle with hearing God? Find a mature believer who hears God and ask him or her to share with you his or her experience in hearing God's voice.*

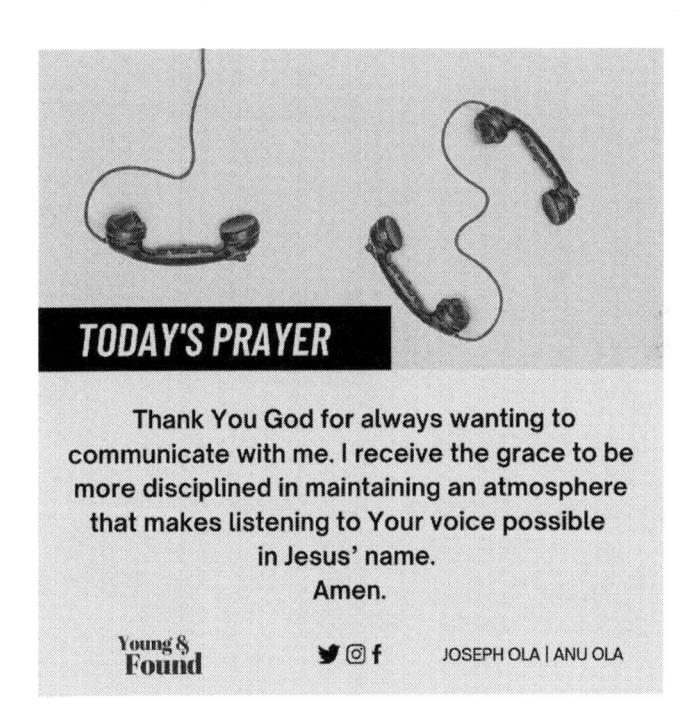

TODAY'S PRAYER

Thank You God for always wanting to communicate with me. I receive the grace to be more disciplined in maintaining an atmosphere that makes listening to Your voice possible in Jesus' name.
Amen.

Young & Found   🐦 📷 f   JOSEPH OLA | ANU OLA

4

ASSUME THE BEST

BY JOSEPH OLA

"Love ... never stops believing the best for others."
(1 Corinthians 13:7 TPT)

The other day while in Bible College, we were having a lecture and I was busy taking down notes on my Chromebook when the lady sitting in front of me decided to palm through her long hair—you know how ladies run their fingers to the base of their hair and throw it back over their head? Well, she did something like that. But unknown to her, she had spilled her hair over my Chromebook screen...

I had about a couple of options: I could get mad at her and rudely fling back the hair. I could even *assume* (and conclude) that she's being insensitive and proud and I could go on and form a negative notion about her... or I could assume she had no idea what she did and that she would apologise if she knew.

What did I do? I gently took her hair off my screen, and as I did she looked back...and she smiled at me. Oh, how lovely! A wrong assumption would have gotten me a frown and not a smile...

Later the same day, a friend said at a small group meeting, *"Love is accepting an apology that was never given."* How true! Paul couldn't have said it better:

> "love knows no limit to its endurance", "always expect the best of someone" and keeps "looking for the best in each one"
>
> — (1 Corinthians 13:7 PHILLIPS, TLB & AMP)

I see you experiencing an increase in your love tank today.

Over to you . . .

- *Is it possible that you are actually experiencing a strain in one of your relationships right now because of an assumption that has not been immersed in love?*
- *Share on social media today: "If you will assume at all, assume the best." #YoungAndFound*

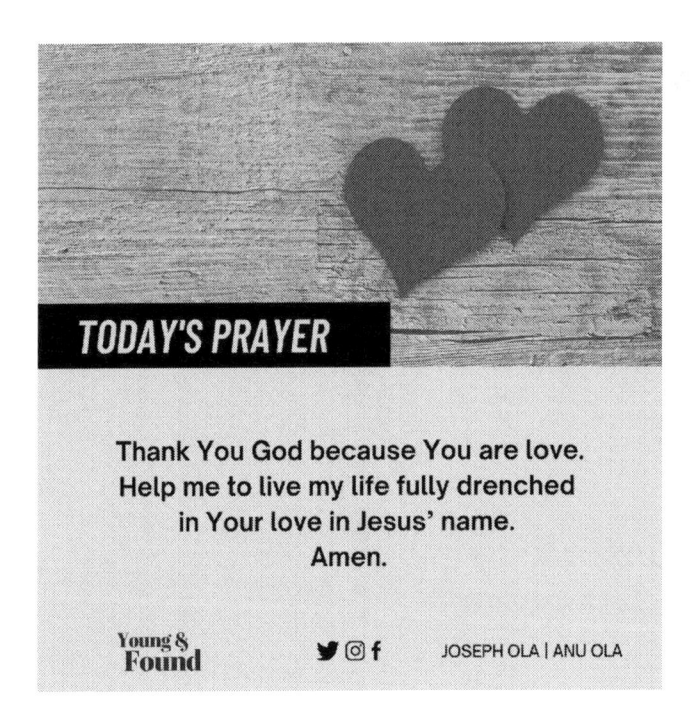

TODAY'S PRAYER

Thank You God because You are love.
Help me to live my life fully drenched
in Your love in Jesus' name.
Amen.

Young & Found   JOSEPH OLA | ANU OLA

5

S-O-A-P IT
BY JOSEPH OLA

"Two can accomplish more than twice as much as one..."
(Ecclesiastes 4:9 TLB)

Having a consistent personal Bible Study devotional pattern is a common challenge for young adults—at least, it was for me. Not that I don't read 'something' from the Bible everyday—that's almost impossible. At least I will stumble on a Facebook post that has a Bible verse . . . or get to read one of the many devotionals that land in my email inbox on daily basis . . . or read a Plan on my Bible app. But while I have a daily interaction with the Bible, I lacked a systematic engagement with

God's Word. My engagement has become more of random coincidence or responsibility than a conscious consistent venture. Until I learnt about S-O-A-P.

SOAP is a Bible Study approach which I tried with my then fiancée (now my wife and mother of our sons). S-O-A-P is an acronym for:

Scripture
Observation
Application
Prayer.

It's better done by at least two people for the sake of accountability and maximal enjoyment. For us, we both choose a passage of **SCRIPTURE** to study individually—the shorter the better. (Tip: We started with Jesus' parables.) After studying the passage individually and journaled our observations, we talk at an appointed time (on the phone) to discuss our **OBSERVATIONS**. We talk about every observation; it doesn't even have to make sense—we just squeeze out everything we can find from the passage—lessons, questions, contradictions etc. Then we link it to issues in our lives—that is **APPLICATION**. Then we wrap it up with a **PRAYER**.

You may want to give it a try with an accountability partner that would be interested. "Two", Bible says, "are better than one."

Over to you . . .

- *Do you already have a personal bible study approach that works for you?*
- *If you will like to consider S-O-A-P, send a message to your potential accountability partner(s) and get started with the challenge.*

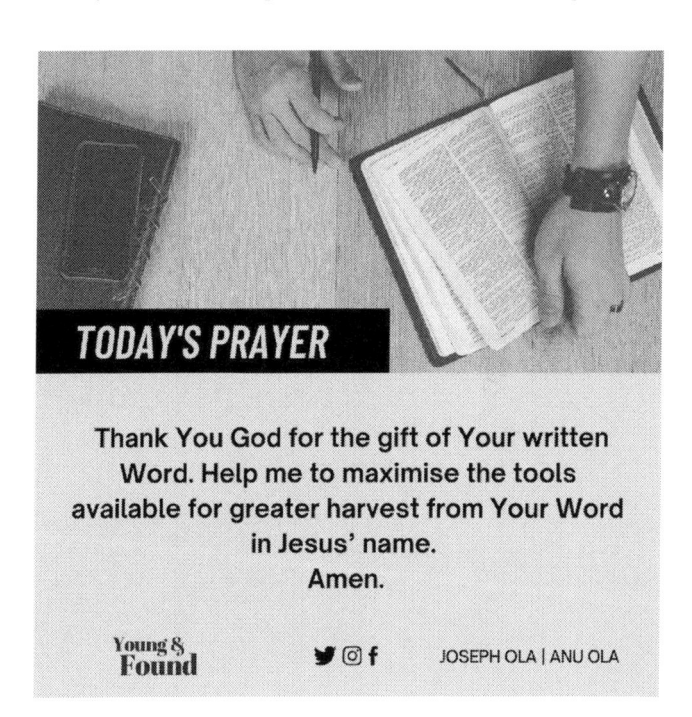

TODAY'S PRAYER

Thank You God for the gift of Your written Word. Help me to maximise the tools available for greater harvest from Your Word in Jesus' name.
Amen.

Young & Found | JOSEPH OLA | ANU OLA

TIME-OUT
BY JOSEPH OLA

*"Are you weary...? Then come to me.
I will refresh your life, for I am your oasis."
(Matthew 11:28 TPT)*

The other day, I woke up feeling aches in different parts of my body. I thought I could pull myself out of the bed, do some bodily exercise, have a cup of tea and set out for the day... or I could consider in retrospect how I'd overstressed my body already, and take a time-out to rest. I chose the latter. I called my leader in the Bible College and requested a permission to be absent.

It's funny that we tend to define diligence and hard work by how quickly we brush aside our exhaustion and by how much we are able to do despite our tiredness. It's commendable in our busy world's perspective, but not from God's. Even in the 10 commandments, while just five English words were enough to condemn adultery; and four to denounce stealing and murder, the command to rest required a paragraph (see Exodus 20:8-11)[1].

I've learnt that in the long run, I do more by doing less. That day, I was able to answer some questions a couple of friends asked me on Facebook more quickly and in more details; I started reading 2 books and glancing through a third; I spent quality time studying God's Word; I cooked some good food, saw a couple of episodes in *The Bible movie* on Netflix, listened to some good music, and stayed alert through the 81 minutes I spent SOAPing with my fiancée that night. In the long run, I did more by doing less!

What's wise is to not wait till you are burning out before taking a time-out. Live a life of strategic and consistent rest. You need it to keep performing at your best. Selah.

Over to you . . .

- *When last did you have an eight-hour sleep?*
- *Challenge yourself to take a Sabbath on one day within the next 7 days whereby you do nothing other than rest, eat and enjoy quality time with your family. (Tip: When you do this, shut down your access to social media, too.)*

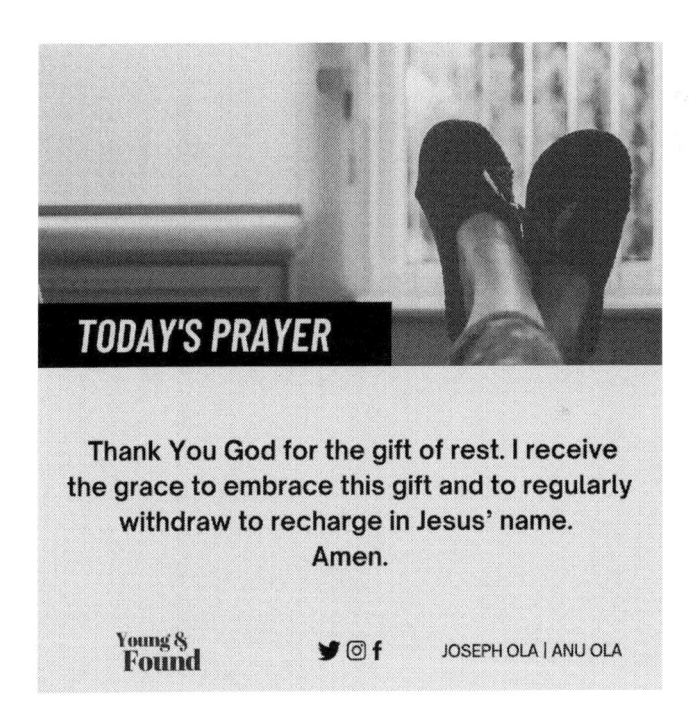

TODAY'S PRAYER

Thank You God for the gift of rest. I receive the grace to embrace this gift and to regularly withdraw to recharge in Jesus' name.
Amen.

Young & Found   JOSEPH OLA | ANU OLA

7

CONFIGURED FOR TOMORROW

BY ANU OLA

I thank you, God, for making me so mysteriously complex! Everything you do is marvelously breathtaking.
It simply amazes me to think about it!
How thoroughly you know me, Lord!
(Psalm 139:14 TPT)

Growing up was wonderful. I became a *matron* at an early age. I could cook, manage the house and my brothers before I knew what boyfriends were. Besides, my brothers made sure I had lots of electronic gadgets to play with. I had an iPad, an iPod, a Bluetooth headphone, and a game station. Yay! Plus, I love reading. It's my favourite pastime till date and my dad made sure I had as many books as I wanted. He gave me money on weekends to buy books. Oh what a joy! Indeed, I grew up with many privileges but chose not to own them. I knew my parents were well-to-do but, subconsciously, I never claimed their wealth. It was something I lived with and saw but never accepted.

Looking back in retrospect, I discovered that it was all a grand plan. The experiences and circumstances of my growing up years shielded me from peer pressure and puberty fever. I was so content running the house that I was blinded to what my age mates were doing. I could have turned out snotty and all snobbish because I had it all but my unique circumstances shaped me in a way that makes me fitted for my current reality today. When I look back now, I'm amazed at God's ingenuity in choosing the family He sent me into—with all their fallibilities—in orchestrating the circumstances that shaped me growing up. All of these were tools which He used masterfully to bring out the best in me and make me ready for today. As a pastor's wife, a young mother and a paralegal today, I bless God for the good, the bad and the ugly of yesteryears.

What are you going through today? Permit me to submit to you that it's all part of God's configuring tools for where you will be tomorrow. Submit wholly to Him.

Over to you . . .

- *Tweet or post this on social media: "Whatever you are going through today is divinely configuring you for tomorrow."*
#YoungAndFound

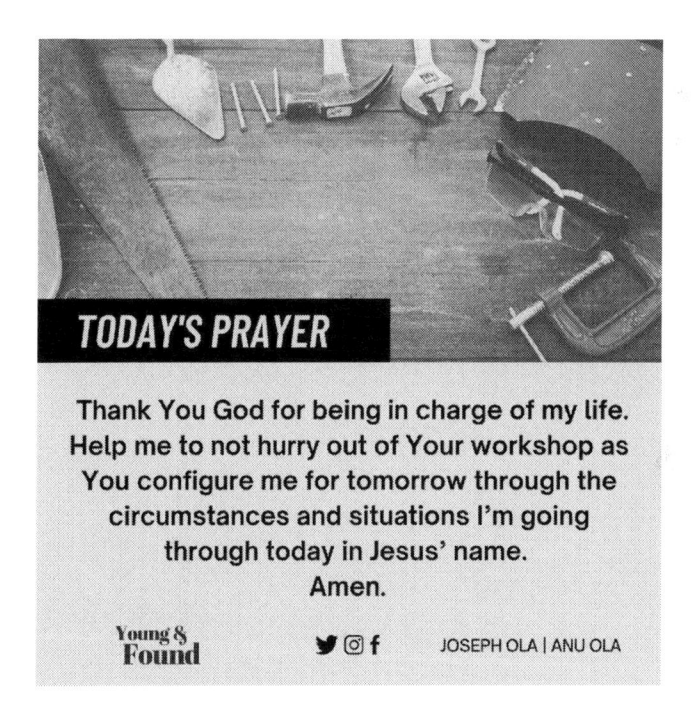

TODAY'S PRAYER

Thank You God for being in charge of my life. Help me to not hurry out of Your workshop as You configure me for tomorrow through the circumstances and situations I'm going through today in Jesus' name.
Amen.

JOSEPH OLA | ANU OLA

8

CASUAL SEX?
BY JOSEPH OLA

"There's more to sex than mere skin on skin.
Sex is as much spiritual mystery as physical fact."
(1 Corinthians 6:16 MSG)

The other day, I was invited to a youth hangout at a pentecostal church in Bradford, UK. Our subject of discussion was sex. We reasoned together about very many things: soul ties, premarital sex, blue balls (I heard that for the first time at that hangout), anal and oral sex, masturbation and the likes. I did more of listening and note taking than talking, so I've decided to share a few of my jottings from the hangout over the next few days:

There's no such thing as casual sex

'Sexual intercourse' is such an apt description for sex. The word 'intercourse' is defined thus:

> communication or dealings between individuals or groups.

Synonyms will include words like *interchange, transactions,* and *bargaining.* Sex is exactly that — an inter-course—an intertwining of two (or more) people's *courses.* The first definition of 'course' that I saw on Google says

> the route or direction...the way in which something progresses or develops.

Hence, an intercourse is a mingling of two people's journeys. It goes without saying that for every such mingling, each participant leaves the *inter-course* not the same way they went into it. You don't make a transaction and still have with you exactly what you take to the bargaining table—despite what Hollywood says. (Ask Esau).

All that to say this: Sex is not something you want to get into with just anybody. Yes, sex is good, but it is best shared with the right person—your lawfully wedded spouse!

Over to you . . .

- *Challenge yourself to compile a list of 'Top 5 lies about sex' according to Hollywood.*
- *Take a moment to meditate on 1 Corinthians 6:16.*

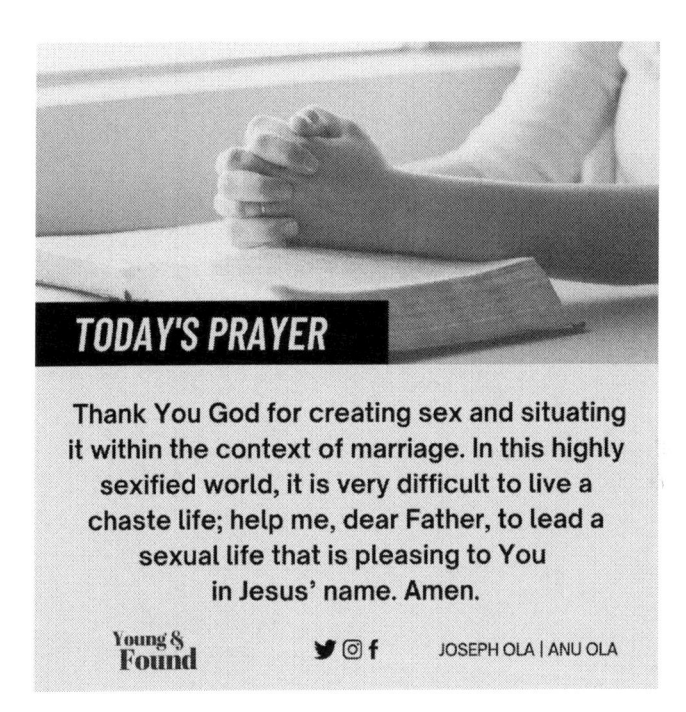

TODAY'S PRAYER

Thank You God for creating sex and situating it within the context of marriage. In this highly sexified world, it is very difficult to live a chaste life; help me, dear Father, to lead a sexual life that is pleasing to You in Jesus' name. Amen.

Young & Found — JOSEPH OLA | ANU OLA

PREMARITAL SEX
BY JOSEPH OLA

"...we must not pursue the kind of sex that avoids commitment and intimacy, leaving us more lonely than ever—the kind of sex that can never "become one.""
(1 Corinthians 6:18 MSG)

Abstain or Desist

As I type this day's devotional, I have just finished reaching out to two friends —*boyfriend* and *girlfriend*. The girl is pregnant and they are yet to be married. The pregnancy prompted them to hasten their wedding plans but planning a wedding in such haste has brought them more disagreements in a few weeks than they have experienced in their one-year of being 'together'. The last I heard from the guy is that he doesn't want to continue with the relationship but he's ready to take responsibility for the unborn child. That's messy, isn't it?

Premarital sex happens on three premises. One is *casual sex* (which we've touched on yesterday), another is *rape* (which we will touch on later in this devotional), and the third is the idea that *"we love each other and are going to be married anyway"*. Let's explore that. What does that mindset highlight? Impatience, for one, besides eroding the extraordinariness of marital relationships. Choosing to make your to-be spouse understand that they're worth waiting for reinforces the relationship and elevates the commitment level of both parties.

Many young people, I've found, nurture their sinful intents under the cloak of friendship. They say *"(s)he's just my friend; there's nothing between us"* yet, they allow themselves to be touched anyhow. Put your friendships to the litmus test of light. If all you do as friends can't be done in the light, such a friendship is unhealthy. You need to admit your deceptions before the chains of your disobedience can be broken.

Abstain. Or if that is no longer an option, desist. And by God's grace, you can.

Over to you . . .

- *Do you struggle with sexual sins or know someone who do? Take some time to pray for the grace (God's ability to do what you can't do on your own) to say no when you (and/or your friend) should.*
- *Ask that God will always open your eyes to see the way of escape out of every sexual temptation.*

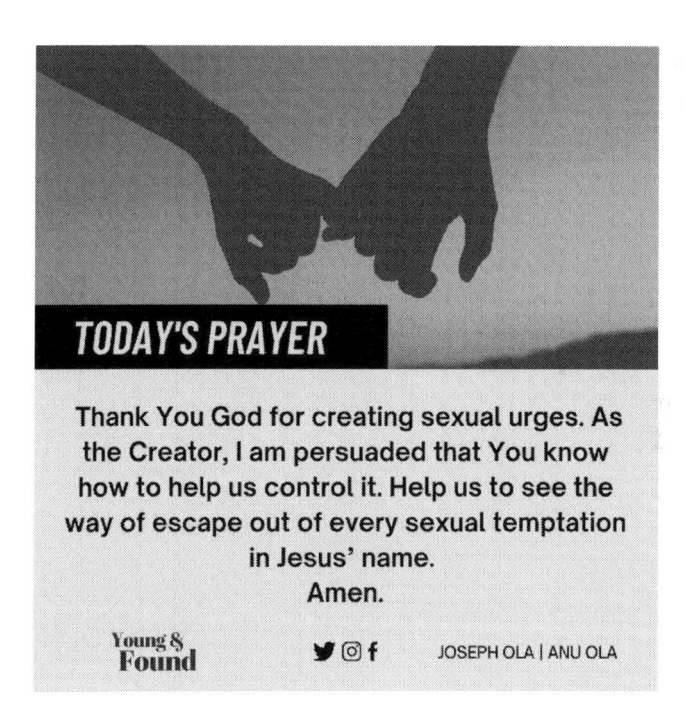

TODAY'S PRAYER

Thank You God for creating sexual urges. As the Creator, I am persuaded that You know how to help us control it. Help us to see the way of escape out of every sexual temptation in Jesus' name.
Amen.

Young & Found　　🐦 ⓘ f　　JOSEPH OLA | ANU OLA

10

I CAN DO BAD ALL BY MYSELF
BY JOSEPH OLA

"...Your heart can be corrupted by lust even quicker than your body. Those leering looks you think nobody notices—they also corrupt."
(Matthew 5:28 MSG)

Masturbation

I find it interesting that less people have asked me, *"Is masturbation a sin?"* than *"How do I break free from a masturbation addiction?"* It tells me that for the most part, many people feel it is sinful. In 2013, I journeyed through *My Beautiful Feeling*—a book written by Walter and Ingrid Trobisch (a compilation of their correspondence exchange with a lady who accidentally stumbled into the act of masturbation) in a private online group with 21 young adults who have one thing in common: a desire to be rid of their addiction to masturbation —an addiction I used to have.

If you or a friend still wonders if masturbation is sinful, the bible didn't say. Maybe masturbation wouldn't have been wrong if people could do it without thinking lustful thoughts to get the process going—but so far, I've found that almost impracticable. And in the words of Jesus,

> if a man looks at a woman and wants to sin sexually with her, he has already committed that sin with her in his mind... Your heart can be corrupted by lust even quicker than your body. Those leering looks you think nobody notices—they also corrupt.
>
> — Matthew 5:28 ERV & MSG

Masturbation almost always stems from lustful thinking, pornography and/or infelicitous sexual stimulation and those are the issues that need to be dealt with to overcome the addiction.

Receive the grace to overcome every shackles of sexual immorality today in Jesus' name.

Over to you . . .

- *Read Matthew 5:28 from different translations of the Bible. How would you think of masturbation in light of that verse?*

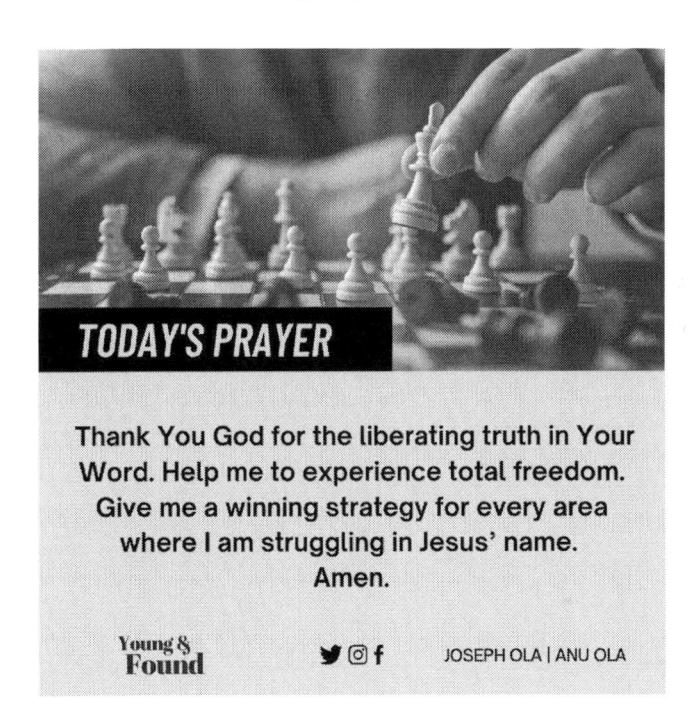

TODAY'S PRAYER

Thank You God for the liberating truth in Your Word. Help me to experience total freedom. Give me a winning strategy for every area where I am struggling in Jesus' name.
Amen.

Young & Found

JOSEPH OLA | ANU OLA

11

#NOSUM
BY JOSEPH OLA

"...if we confess our sins, he will forgive our sins, because we can trust God to do what is right. He will cleanse us from all the wrongs we have done."
(1 John 1:9 NCV)

A 19-year-old lady read the analogy below illustrating the disadvantages of premarital sex:

> If we glue one object to another, it will adhere. If we remove it, it will leave behind a small amount of residue; the longer it remains, the more residue is left. If we take that glued object

and stick it to several places repeatedly, it will leave residue everywhere we stick it, and it will eventually lose its ability to adhere to anything. This is much like what happens to us when we engage in *casual* sex. Each time we leave a sexual relationship, we leave a part of ourselves behind. The longer the relationship has gone on, the more we leave behind, and the more we lose of ourselves. As we go from partner to partner, we continue to lose a tiny bit of ourselves each time, and eventually we may lose our ability to form a lasting sexual relationship at all.

She felt convicted by the analogy and wanted to know if there is still any hope for her. I asked her, *"Is there any sin the blood of Christ did not pay for?"* The answer is none. When we confess our sins, He is faithful and just to forgive us *and* to cleanse us from all our unrighteousness (see 1 John 1:9).[1] That which we have lost in sticking to all manner of surfaces, the Lord is able to restore in a manner like He alone can and to the praise of His glory alone.

Irrespective of the occurrences of your past—yes, you may have had sex before now and marriage may still be a while away—it's never too late to join the no-sex-*until*-marriage campaign (#NOSUM).

May you grow continually in chastity.

Over to you . . .

- *Share a post on social media today using the hashtags #NOSUM and #YoungAndFound*

TODAY'S PRAYER

Dad, to You Who has enough power to prevent me from stumbling into sin and to bring me faultless before Your glorious presence to stand before You with ecstatic delight—to You alone I commit my life. Help me. Keep me. Preserve me. And direct me—now and forever more in Jesus' name. Amen.

Young & Found   JOSEPH OLA | ANU OLA

12

HONOUR YOUR PARENTS
BY ANU OLA

Honor your father and mother. This is the first of God's Ten Commandments that ends with a promise.
(Ephesians 6:2 TLB)

I come from a very conservative family. My parents are not shouty; they simply don't show off or maybe show off in a conservative way. So, I have learnt to be like that. We don't do birthday parties or any parties at that. My dad (of blessed memory) believed every day should be celebrated and no day was extra special. *So, calm your horses Aanu?*

However, since I came to the UK, I get calls from my uncle reminding me to be the first person to wish my parents a happy birthday on their birthdays . . . or that I should not forget to send some money to them occasionally. I tried explaining to him that we don't roll like that in my family. My parents don't *need* anything from me; they are well established. Reluctantly, few years ago, I decided to take my uncle's advice and called my mom very early on her birthday to wish her a happy birthday. And she loved it! I was confused. I wanted to ask her what would have happened if I had forgotten to call but I got lost in the happy feeling of being appreciated. So my uncle was right, after all.

I have learnt that honour is such a big thing, more so for our parents. My idea of honour is to pray silently in my mind for my parents or call them or put their pictures on my WhatsApp DP. And every now and again, I go out of my way and unique peculiarities to honour them. We won't always have our parents with us. We must not allow the illusion of post-modernism rob us of a blessing that God promised to those who honour their parents. "You will prosper and live a long, full life *if you honor your parents.*" (Ephesians 6:3 TPT).

It may not be the way we want it or expect it to be, but we must try as much as possible to make sure we celebrate the parents that groomed us. And since they are the recipients of our honour, we must observe them and understand how they will like to be honoured, and then do it.

Over to you . . .

- *Do something that expresses honour to your parent(s) or the parental figures in your life today. (Tip: It could be as a simple phone call to let them know you are thinking of them, or send them a token.)*

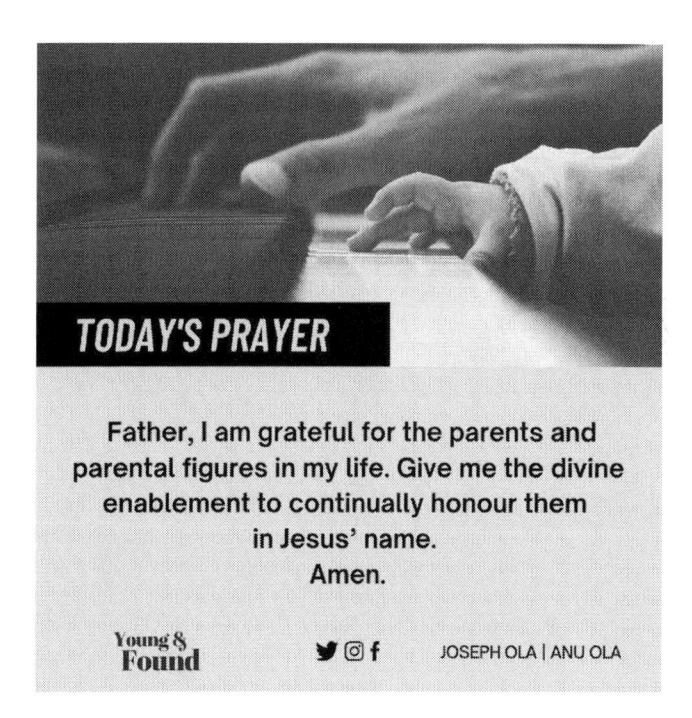

TODAY'S PRAYER

Father, I am grateful for the parents and parental figures in my life. Give me the divine enablement to continually honour them in Jesus' name.
Amen.

Young & Found   JOSEPH OLA | ANU OLA

13

ATTITUDE IS EVERYTHING
BY JOSEPH OLA

"A cheerful disposition is good for your health;
gloom and doom leave you bone-tired."
(Proverbs 17:22 MSG)

In April 2016, three months before our wedding, my then-fiancée and I had many pleasantly difficult conversations while reading *The Act of Marriage* together. We read a chapter a day and discussed the chapter over a phone conversation each night. We wanted to glean from the wisdom of Tim and Beverly LaHaye (who had both been married for over 70 years!)

One of our major takeaways from reviewing the book together is that *attitude is everything!* In human relations, in your academics, in your spiritual life, in your dieting, in how you treat your body, and for your information, in what your sexual life will look like when you get married.

Keeping a positive attitude is fundamental to living the life God intended for each of us and His Spirit that dwells in us empowers us with hope and optimism—the secret ingredients for positive attitude.

When we let Him, the Holy Spirit helps us to see the good in every difficulty and as we keep looking for something good or beneficial in a person or situation, we become more positive and cheerful.

Resolve from today to start seeing your glass of life as half full rather than half empty. Resolve to be cheerful, no matter what happens. "If you are cheerful, you feel good; if you are sad, you hurt all over." (Proverbs 17:22 CEV)

I see you having a blissful marriage in the nearest future.

Over to you . . .

- *Ask two or three honest inner-circle friends what they think about your attitude and how you can improve on it.*

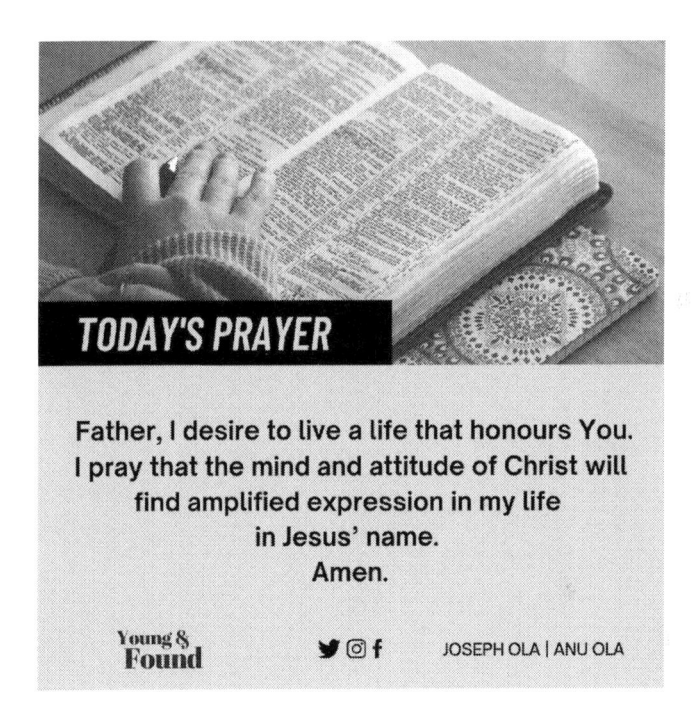

TODAY'S PRAYER

**Father, I desire to live a life that honours You. I pray that the mind and attitude of Christ will find amplified expression in my life in Jesus' name.
Amen.**

Young & Found JOSEPH OLA | ANU OLA

14

FROM FEAR TO FAITH (1)
BY JOSEPH OLA

"for your God is the supreme God of heaven, not just an ordinary god."
(Joshua 2:11 TLB)

The other day, I attended a youth group meeting where the lives of Rahab and Tabitha were discussed. Of the two, Rahab's story fascinated me more because of the many questions it raises:

- *What kind of a woman was she for her to command such influence in her extended family despite being a renowned prostitute?* (She didn't seek salvation from the pending war for herself alone but for the whole family.)

- *What exactly is the reason why she "got saved"—was it her fear or her faith?*

In her own words, she said to the spies,

> **...we are all afraid of you; everyone is terrified if the word 'Israel' is even mentioned.** For **we have heard** how the Lord made a path through the red sea for you when you left Egypt! and **we know** what you did to Sihon and Og...**no one has any fight left in him after hearing things like that, for your God is the supreme God** of heaven, not just an ordinary god...
>
> — Joshua 2:8-11 TLB

You keep hearing her make reference to words like 'afraid' and 'terrified'. In a sense, it does sound like she was seeking salvation because she was scared, yet she was referenced in other places (even in the Hebrew 11 hall of fame) as someone who had faith. Apparently, she didn't stop at being scared of the God of Israel—it's only common sense to be afraid of One that could part a sea and lead multitude through the same on dry ground. But more importantly, she allowed her fear to lead her to faith.

With her own mouth, she proclaimed *"...for your God is the Supreme God of heaven, not just an ordinary God..."*

Don't stop at Fear Avenue. Move on to Faith Lane.

Over to you . . .

- *What are you afraid of right now?*
- *How can you turn that fear into faith? (Tip: Faith comes from hearing God's Word. Let what you are afraid of lead you to dig up what God has said about it in His Word . . . and as such, faith will arise!)*

TODAY'S PRAYER

Father, I choose to stand upon Your promises. I declare that I have not received the spirit of fear but of power, love and a sound mind in Jesus' name.
Amen.

JOSEPH OLA | ANU OLA

15

FROM FEAR TO FAITH (2)
BY JOSEPH OLA

*Jesus said "Thomas, don't give in to your doubts any longer, just believe!" Then the words spilled **out of his heart**—*
"You are my Lord, and you are my God!""
(John 20:27-28 TPT)

Rahab's story which we considered yesterday also reminds me of Thomas'. He doubted Jesus' resurrection until he had a personal proof. But when he did, he made a solid proclamation that has become central to the individuality of receiving Salvation:

"You are MY Lord and MY God…"

Their story reminds me of ours. I've spoken with believers that were saved more out of fear (or doubt) than out of faith. More out of not wanting to go to hell than wanting to have a relationship with God. In fact, I've been there. And for some of us, our cultural backdrop makes it worse. As such, we keep seeing God through the lenses of how we see our earthly father (someone that can be friendly occasionally and fiery when we mess up).

But may I suggest to you that it's okay to come to Christ motivated by fear or doubt ... but don't stop there. Draw nearer. Look deeper. Ponder harder. Until the light breaks in your thinking and the illumination thereof liberates your heart and opens its gates to such undiluted Love that beckons anyone and everyone to come.

The goal of our salvation is to have a relationship with God in Christ so much so that we become like Christ. It's okay to have been saved because you didn't want to go to hell, but hell is too tiny a motivation for all that awaits you in Christ! Embrace the right motivation—the untold beauties of being in a living relationship with God—and your day-to-day experiences will take on a new joy!

Over to you . . .

- *Have you made the choice to live for Jesus?*
- *If you have, what was your motivation?*
- *Share the good news of your salvation experience with someone today.*

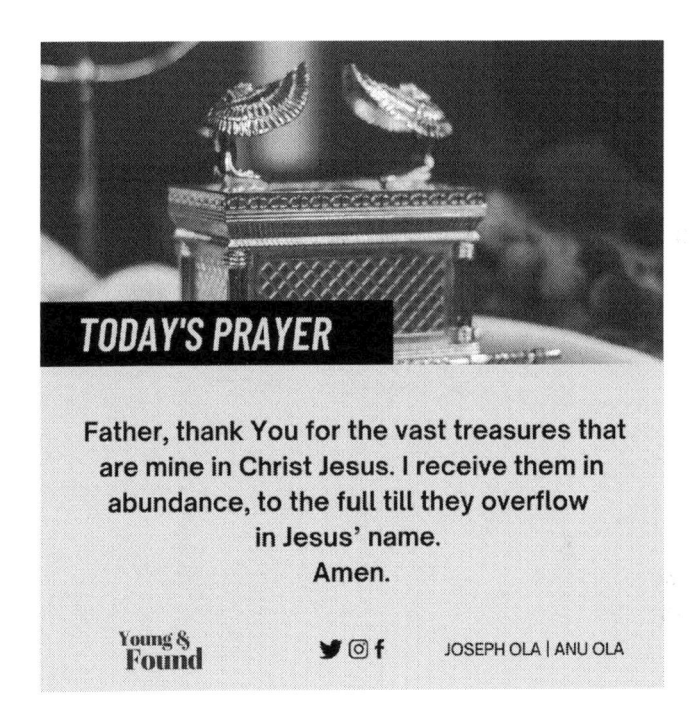

TODAY'S PRAYER

Father, thank You for the vast treasures that are mine in Christ Jesus. I receive them in abundance, to the full till they overflow in Jesus' name.
Amen.

Young & Found

JOSEPH OLA | ANU OLA

16

JUSTIFIED CHEATING?
BY JOSEPH OLA

"Love takes no pleasure in other people's sins
but delights in the truth"
(1 Corinthians 13:6 JB)

While in college, I had a friend who had some difficulty writing essays in English because English was not her first (or second) language. She requested that I help her by sending her the soft copies of mine so she could tweak it and resubmit as hers. As I stared at my computer screen about to send the files, I had conflicting thoughts...

> *"You are helping her...she doesn't understand English...it's called love. Send it!"*
>
> *"No, that's cheating... Both of you could be penalised... Don't tarnish your image because of a lady's feminine charm..."*

The voices were so conflicting that all I thought to do was sleep. When I woke up the next day, my head was clear enough to know the right thing to say to her.

> Hey! Why don't you let's discuss the assignment together maybe early in the morning on Saturday, so that I can explain it to you rather than just sending you the one I did? Will that be okay? I will stay with you and even help you type if need be...

And that was it. Together, we went through the assignments and I helped her through without having to break the rules.

The message: There is no justification for cheating!

> Love does not delight in evil but rejoices with the truth.
>
> — 1 Corinthians 13:6 NIV

If you want to weigh your action in a friendship on the scale of love, ask yourself this: *"Do I encourage this person to do what is right?"* True love, Paul says, "takes no pleasure in other people's sins but delights in the truth" (1 Corinthians 13:6 JB). If you find yourself prompting or promoting evil in others, heed the alarm. That is not love. And if others prompt or promote evil in you, be alert. Troubleshoot your sincerity.

Over to you . . .

- *Have you got a similar story about (almost) cheating? Share it with someone today to encourage them to go for integrity.*

TODAY'S PRAYER

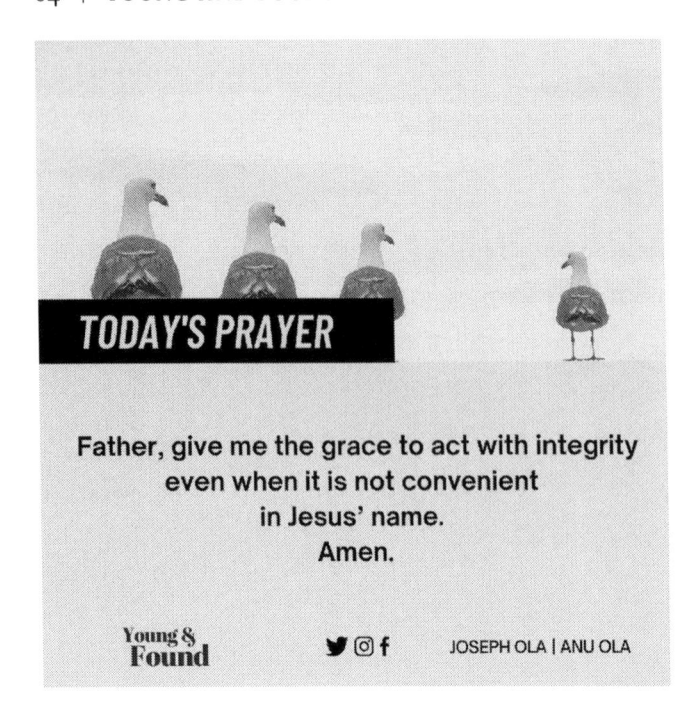

Father, give me the grace to act with integrity even when it is not convenient in Jesus' name.
Amen.

Young & Found

JOSEPH OLA | ANU OLA

17

MUTUAL SUBMISSION
BY ANU OLA

Submit yourselves to one another because of your reverence for Christ. (Ephesians 5:21 GNT)

Submission remains a touchy subject, more so among young ladies who are trying to be both Christian and feminist at the same time—and I believe you can be both, depending on how you define those terms. However, rather than get caught up with the implications or exposition of Ephesians 5:23 where wives are enjoined to submit to their husbands, I think a simple understanding of what submission means—mutually for that matter—will help to put things in perspective. To do this, I will simply employ a few translations to get a grip of what submission entails.

- "Honor Christ and put others first." — CEV
- "Be willing to serve each other out of respect for Christ." — ERV
- "Place yourselves under each other's authority out of respect for Christ." — GW
- "Be willing to obey each other. Do this because you respect Christ." — ICB
- "And "fit in with" each other, because of your common reverence for Christ." — PHILLIPS
- "Out of respect for Christ, be courteously reverent to one another." — MSG
- "Yield to obey each other as you would to Christ." — NCV
- "Follow the lead of one another because of your respect for Christ." — NIRV
- "Be willing to help and care for each other because of Christ. By doing this, you honor Christ." — NLV
- "And out of your reverence for Christ be supportive of each other in love." — TPT
- "Give way to each other because you respect Christ." — WE

To put it simply, submission is deferring to one another. Plainly speaking, it is a first a mutual virtue before it is demanded of wives in a marital context. If we have lived our lives putting others before ourselves, serving them out of respect, being courteously reverent to them, following their lead and being willing to help and care for them, submission in marriage won't be a big deal.

Over to you . . .

- *Which of those versions of Ephesians 5:21 resonates most with you?*
- *Write it out or copy and share it on social media using #YoungAndFound*

TODAY'S PRAYER

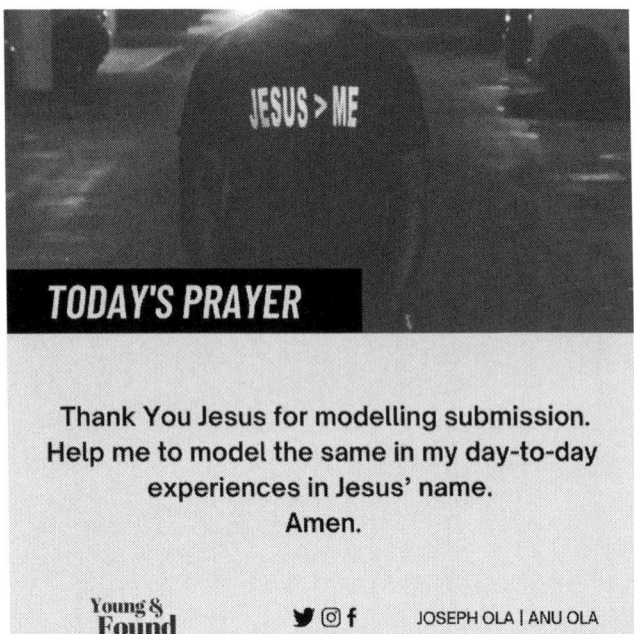

Thank You Jesus for modelling submission. Help me to model the same in my day-to-day experiences in Jesus' name.
Amen.

Young & Found

JOSEPH OLA | ANU OLA

18

ENJOY LIFE
BY JOSEPH OLA

"...the Son of Man came, enjoying life..."
(Matthew 11:19 PHILLIPS)

One of my favourite days while I was in Bible College in Bradford had nothing to do with 'Bible'. It was a 'Naija Evening' hosted by one of the 3 other Nigerians in my class. When we got together during lunch breaks or even in-between lectures, our talks tend to quickly drift to jollof rice and Nollywood movies. So one of us decided to organise a 'Naija Evening' in her house to mark her 22nd birthday. 3 of us turned up and it was really a great evening! We listened to Nigerian songs on YouTube, had some Nigerian food and drink, and watched a Nollywood movie (of which we spent half an hour analysing the production flaws). In all, we had a lot of fun!

The message: As a Christian, no matter the level you get to spiritually, never forget to make out some time for enjoying life! Your conscience is clear, so enjoy life. You are secure within God's love, so enjoy life. Give yourself a belly laugh sometimes. Having surrounded yourself with friends who don't manipulate you—enjoy their friendship.

Even of Jesus, John writes:

> ...the Son of man came, *enjoying life*...
>
> — Matthew 11:19 PHILLIPS

And Paul tells Timothy that God "richly provides us with everything *for our enjoyment*" (1 Timothy 6:17b NIV). You may be under a lot of stress right now because of the economy, but God still wants you to enjoy life.

As you ride elegantly into the rest of your life, do so enjoying life!

Over to you . . .

- *Include one fun thing in your schedule for today or tomorrow — and do it. (Tip: Watch a movie with a friend; go hiking; go to a place you've never been before; eat out — or any other fun thing you can think about.)*

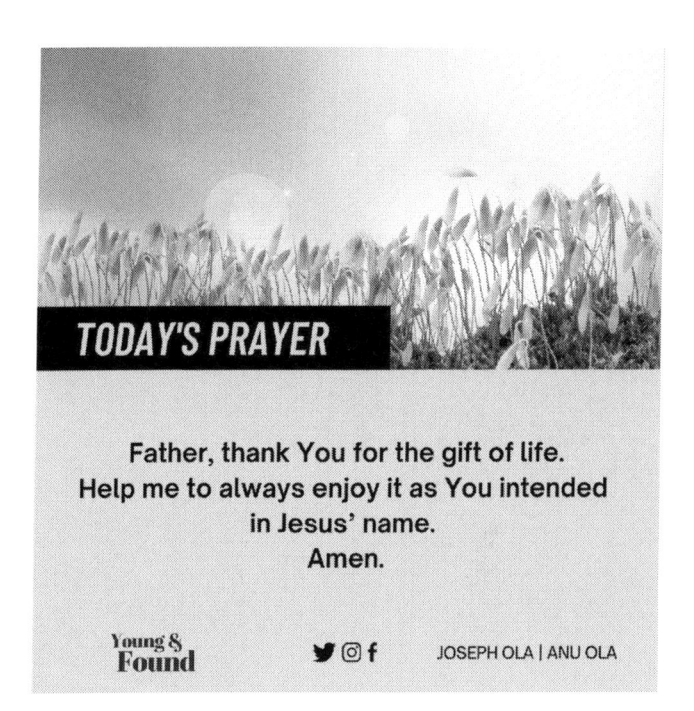

TODAY'S PRAYER

Father, thank You for the gift of life.
Help me to always enjoy it as You intended
in Jesus' name.
Amen.

Young & Found

JOSEPH OLA | ANU OLA

19

WE ARE ALL TEACHERS
BY JOSEPH OLA

"...Your very lives are a letter that anyone can read by just looking at you."
(2 Corinthians 3:2 MSG)

It was a beautiful April evening in 2016. Walking ahead of me was this young dad and his little boy. No doubt, they were having a lovely dad-son time. We arrived at the main road at the same time—a 5-lane motorway with 4 traffic-light moderated pedestrian crossings. When the traffic light gave us a go, we crossed from lane 1 to 2. Then from 2 to 3, and 3 to 4. But in crossing lane 5, I didn't wait for the green light; I just crossed because no car was coming. But after walking for a few paces, I observed that I was walking alone so I looked back to the father-and-son to be sure that all was well with them. Then I saw the father, still holding on to his son and still waiting for the green light, even though no car was coming still.

That was when what I'd done dawned on me. The father was trying to teach his little kid the correct road-user experience and my actions might just have messed up the lesson for the little man. If that boy was able to talk, he probably would have asked his dad why they were still standing at the crossing while I crossed. I must have introduced a little conflict into a little boy's mind and I felt bad about it.

The point is that we are all teachers. Someone somewhere is observing you and will be making some life decisions based on a pattern they've learnt from you. Paul wrote to the Corinthian congregation,

> "Your very lives are a letter that anyone can read by just looking at you..."
>
> — 2 Corinthian 3:2 MSG

Consciously take decisions that will communicate the truth in love to your "readers" and be extra-

We Are All Teachers | 75

careful when you are around very young lads—you are training the next generation!

Over to you . . .

- *Write "I'm a Teacher" in your daily journal. You can even make an artwork with that caption—something to remind you of this precious truth.*

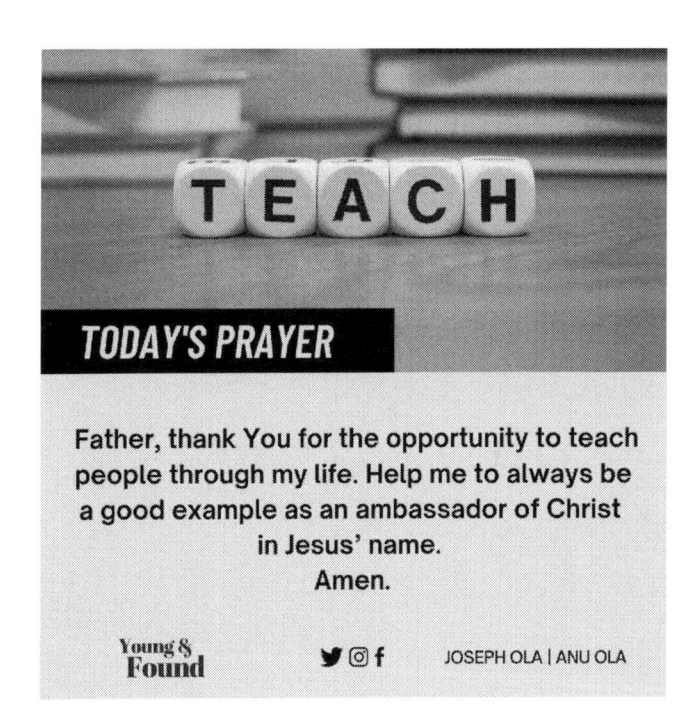

TODAY'S PRAYER

Father, thank You for the opportunity to teach people through my life. Help me to always be a good example as an ambassador of Christ in Jesus' name.
Amen.

Young & Found

JOSEPH OLA | ANU OLA

20

THERE'S AN "ANGEL" IN YOU!
BY JOSEPH OLA

"Don't hide your light! Let it shine for all; let your good deeds glow for all to see..."
(Matthew 5:16 TLB)

A doctor-friend shared an experience with me the other day. It was one of those days when she couldn't wait to clock out, but she got called to insert a cannula into a terminally ill patient. Their conversation went thus:

> **Gentleman:** *Do you really have to put in this line?*
> **Doctor:** (with a sad smiley face) *I'm afraid I need to so you can have your medications.*

(The gentleman reluctantly agrees and closes his eyes.)

Doctor: (whispering) *Holy Spirit, please help me. I don't want to have to prick this man more than once...*

(Indeed, the doctor got it in the first time.)

Gentleman: *Doctor, can you find a vein?*

Doctor: *Oh yes I'm all done.*

Gentleman: *Really? You are an angel! I didn't feel the slightest pinch! You are truly an angel; each time you need to do anything with me I do not feel any pain...*

Doctor: (smiling) *Thank you sir.*

Gentleman: *You truly are. When I get to heaven I will specifically ask God to put a cross on your forehead and watch over you.* (He leans over to get the doctor's badge and finds her name.) *I wish everyone could be like you...*

Doctor: (wipes tears) *Thank you sir.*
(Smiling amidst tears as she walks away thanking her Senior Partner, the Holy Spirit.)

Lesson learnt. Shine your light![1] As a Christian, you have the Spirit of God in you; there's an "angel" in you! It's your choice to let others see it. Show Him to someone today.

There's an "Angel" in You! | 79

Over to you . . .

- *Pray that even your little gestures today will be as a shining light pointing people to Jesus.*

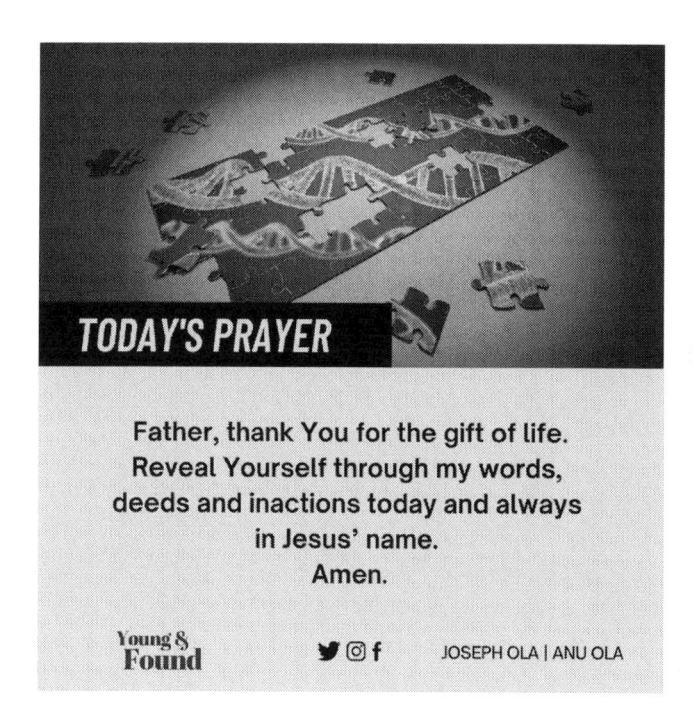

TODAY'S PRAYER

Father, thank You for the gift of life.
Reveal Yourself through my words,
deeds and inactions today and always
in Jesus' name.
Amen.

Young & Found   JOSEPH OLA | ANU OLA

21

HONOUR GOD'S SERVANTS
BY JOSEPH OLA

"The pastors who lead the church well should be paid well. They should receive double honor for faithfully preaching and teaching the revelation of the Word of God."
(1 Timothy 5:17 TPT)

While volunteering at a church office in Bradford, a pastor came visiting from Portsmouth—a 6-hour trip on the train. After checking him into the hotel room booked for him, the host pastor and I asked for what he would like to have for dinner. *"Anything will be fine"*, he said at first, then he smiled and added *"pounded yam will be great"*. He said it teasingly, thinking there's no way we could get pounded yam in Bradford at that time of the day.

The host pastor and I set out on a pounded yam hunting mission. The visiting pastor could not believe it when we returned with the bounty half an hour later—*pounded yam and egusi soup* with assorted meat and fish. His heart blessed us, and so did his mouth. As we were about to take our exits, he said *"God bless you for honouring me; God shall honour you, too."*

That prayer made my day. I got back home much later than any other weekend but more satisfied than most previous weekends. I gave honour to whom honour is due—and that was enough.

Of course, men of God are men like us, but scriptures teach us they are worthy of double honour.

> ...Believe firmly in God, your God, and your lives will be firm! Believe in your prophets and you'll come out on top!
>
> — 2 Chronicles 20:20 MSG

Not because you believe in the prophets for themselves, but because you are honouring God in their lives.

Honour God's Servants | 83

May you come out on top. Amen.

Over to you . . .

- *Think of a creative way to honour your pastor this week. It doesn't have to be something grand; it could be as simple as making a thoughtful remark when next you see him or her.*

TODAY'S PRAYER

Father, thank You for the pastors and ministers You have blessed the body of Christ with. Help me to always You in their lives and to constantly remember them in my prayers in Jesus' name.
Amen.

Young & Found JOSEPH OLA | ANU OLA

22

SUBMISSION IN MARRIAGE
BY ANU OLA

Wives, understand and support your husbands in ways that show your support for Christ. The husband provides leadership to his wife the way Christ does to his church, not by domineering but by cherishing. So just as the church submits to Christ as he exercises such leadership, wives should likewise submit to their husbands.
(Ephesians 5:22-24 MSG)

What does submission look like in my current context as a young wife? It looks like deferring to my husband; running the littlest decision by him first; praising his prowess; cooking when I don't feel like eating; liking his passions;

putting him first before anyone else (including myself). And what does submission look like to my partner in his current context, too? It looks like opening the car door for me when no one is looking; carrying the heaviest luggage so I can be with our son; waiting for me to come home before having dinner; walking me to the bus stop to catch a bus to work—and running with me so I am not late...

Do you notice a recurring theme in those examples above? **Submission is being selfless—and being selfless is love.** To submit is to intentionally deny yourself of the rights and privileges that are justifiably yours; laying down your life as it were. It is being attuned to another's needs. Submission is support.

Before I met my husband, I have always yearned for a relationship where I can be best friends with my partner—the rough-play kind of friendship. But that does not acknowledge the respect that has been culturally ingrained into my system. Then I met Kola and got resigned. He is the best example of a traditional man. He's so hardcore! I felt I had no chance. So I started ridding myself of my childish fantasies and accepted what I got. To my surprise, however, my husband turned out to be meeting my exact expectations without any nagging from my end (which is a miracle by the way).

What's my point? Submission is observing the receiver and giving them what *they* understand submission to be. It is not what *you* call it, it is what *they* call it. It is complete selflessness without expecting anything back. And while our stories, our limits and our outlook might differ, submission affects us all—and it's Christlikeness at its peak.

Over to you . . .

- *Do something selfless today.*
- *(Tips: Give up your seat in a public bus or train; Let the person behind you on the queue go first; accept to take a group photograph even if it means not being in the shot yourself . . . etc.)*

TODAY'S PRAYER

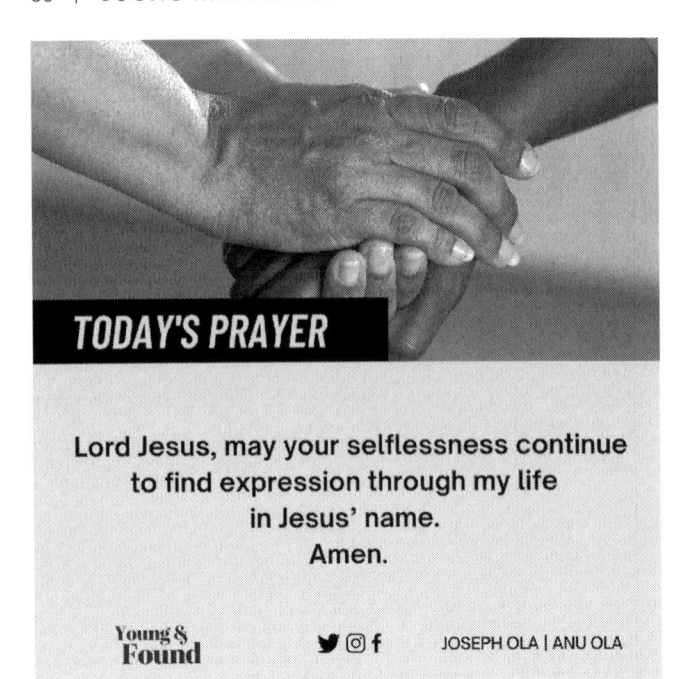

Lord Jesus, may your selflessness continue
to find expression through my life
in Jesus' name.
Amen.

Young & Found JOSEPH OLA | ANU OLA

23

WE ALL HAVE ISSUES
BY JOSEPH OLA

"...my weakness becomes a portal to God's power."
(2 Corinthians 12:10 TPT)

The movie *The King's Speech* retells the story of King George VI (Queen Elizabeth's dad). King George was a stammerer, and as such, the movie highlights the fact that even big and powerful men have issues.

Apostle Paul could relate. In 2 Corinthians 12:1-10, we were notified that despite all of Paul's ministerial exploits, he also had an issue—a *'thorn in the flesh'*. Epilepsy? Running eyes? Migraine? We were not told. But this much we know:

1. God used Paul in spite of his issue.
2. Paul leaned on God's sufficient grace to navigate life with his issue.

Truth is, we all have issues! The masturbation addiction you can't break, the once-in-a-while bed-wetting experience that is embarrassing for you at your age (I experienced that till I gained admission to University), the bow leg you are not proud of, the recurrent sickness, the monthly terrible menstrual pain, the vulnerability to a certain temptation you've not been able to master, the low self-esteem from yesteryear's abuse, the heartbreak you've caused etc.

Thorns love to attach themselves to people making a difference. For every great vision, there comes big thorns. There is no hero in the Bible without his/her own issue. But as much as Paul understood the power of his weakness, he also understood the strength of God. Your strength is found in identifying a weakness and having the humility to face God and say *"I can't handle this on my own."*

Will you?

Over to you . . .

- *What are the 'thorns' in your flesh?*
- *Ask God to show you how your weakness can become a portal to God's power.*

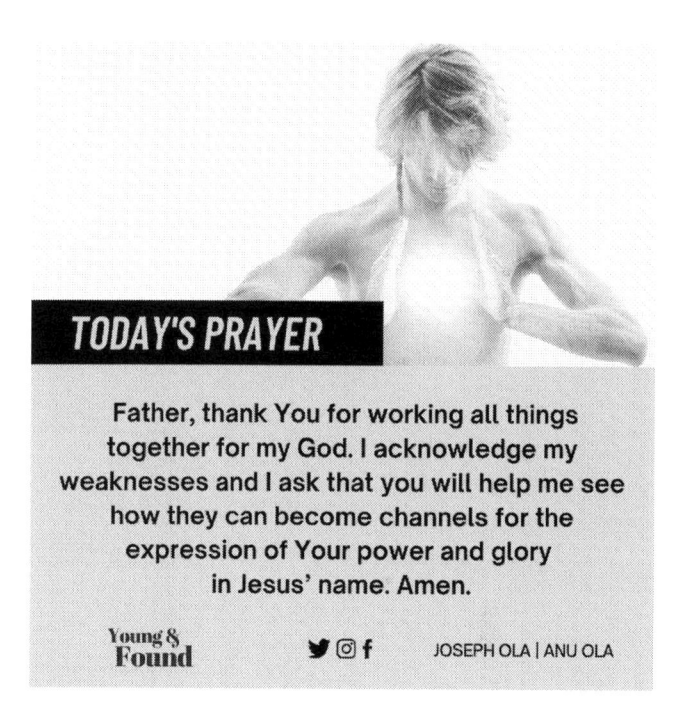

TODAY'S PRAYER

Father, thank You for working all things together for my God. I acknowledge my weaknesses and I ask that you will help me see how they can become channels for the expression of Your power and glory in Jesus' name. Amen.

Young & Found

JOSEPH OLA | ANU OLA

24

YOUR WEAKNESS IS NOT THE ISSUE
BY JOSEPH OLA

"...I quit focusing on the handicap and began appreciating the gift..."
(2 Corinthians 12:9 MSG)

Roses are beautiful and they smell lovely, no doubt, but their stem is full of thorns! In actual fact, however, the thorns of the rose is its protection from preys. Likewise, for Paul; the thorn in his flesh was his protection from pride. And most certainly, yours, too, is a protection from something.

Your weakness is not the issue, the main issue is your reliance upon the grace of God. If you know how strong your weakness is, then endeavour to know how stronger God's Grace is. Soak yourself in the ocean of His sufficient grace till, like Paul, you can say *"I boast about my weaknesses."* Indeed, the weaker you are, the stronger you actually are.

Your weakness doesn't disqualify you but rather distinguishes you. Don't allow your weakness to take you down the streets of self-sufficiency and independence. Doing so will only take you deeper and deeper into its grip. No! We were made to depend on God. By grace, we are saved, and by grace we will be kept saved. I love that line in Wesley's hymn:

> *'Tis grace has brought me safe thus far.*
> *And grace will lead me home.*

Meditate on 2 Corinthians 12:8-10 and ponder Paul's reasoning regarding his weakness—his thorn in the flesh:

> At first I didn't think of (my weakness) as a gift, and begged God to remove it. Three times I did that, and then he told me, My grace is enough; it's all you need. My strength comes into its own in your weakness.Once I heard that, I was glad to let it happen. I quit focusing on the handicap

and began appreciating the gift... Now I take limitations in stride, and with good cheer, these limitations that cut me down to size—abuse, accidents, opposition, bad breaks. I just let Christ take over! And so **the weaker I get, the stronger I become.**

May that be our shared testimony.

Over to you . . .

- *Tweet or share this on social media today: "My weakness is a gift; I will unpack it. So help me God." #YoungAndFound*

TODAY'S PRAYER

Father, thank You for Your great plans for my life. Help me to see the gift in my weaknesses and to unwrap them in the grip of Your grace in Jesus' name.
Amen.

JOSEPH OLA | ANU OLA

YOU NEVER KNOW
BY JOSEPH OLA

"Whatever your hand finds to do, do it with all your might..." (Ecclesiastes 9:10 NIV)

Femi and I went to the same secondary school in Nigeria between 1999 and 2003. He left Nigeria for the UK in our fourth year (SS1). We never saw each other again till 2016 at a valentine dinner where I was scheduled to speak. We sat at the same table. I sat next to my fiancée and he was on the other side of the table. He spotted me, recognised me (I couldn't have recognised him, he looked so different) and we reconnected. We had a little chat, took a selfie to show our old friends, and exchanged numbers. We met again at a Youth

Group few days later and he shared vividly all he could remember about me with the rest of the group. He drove me to my house afterwards and we bade each other farewell. It was a good evening altogether mainly because all that he remembered about me were pleasant things—and that's actually where I'm going: you never know...

You never know where you will meet the people in your life at the moment again. You never know whose car you will be riding in to your house in the next few years. You never know the extent to which your little acts of kindness today can go. You never know who will read tomorrow what you are posting flippantly today.

> Whatever your hand finds to do, do it with all your might...
>
> — Ecclesiastes 9:10 NIV

Whatever *neighbours* you have to love, love them with all your sincerity.

> Whatever you do, put your whole heart and soul into it, as into work done for God, and not merely for men—knowing that your real

reward, a heavenly one, will come from God, since you are actually employed by Christ...

— COLOSSIANS 3:23 PHILLIPS

Why? Because you never know...

Over to you . . .

- *Have you ever had such a reunion like the one described in today's episode? How did that play out?*
- *Go out of your way to do a deed for which you can't be repaid to someone you will meet today (or tomorrow).*

TODAY'S PRAYER

Father, thank You for the friendships in my life. Help me to love people sincerely and to always put my whole heart into whatever I'm doing—to the praise and glory of Your name in Jesus' name.
Amen.

JOSEPH OLA | ANU OLA

SECRET PRAYERS
BY JOSEPH OLA

*"...Pray to your Father in private.
He knows what is done in private, and he will reward you."*
(Matthew 6:6 CEV)

I remember being at a worship gathering and spotting a friend few rows ahead. She's as godly and dedicated as anyone can be and she's old enough to be married but, as she said to me few days earlier, *"no guy comes around"*. Suddenly, at the worship event, I found myself praying passionately for her as if my life depended on that prayer—that God will bring her into the awareness of *"the one"* and bring *"the one"* into an awareness of her...

Looking back in retrospect, I felt very fulfilled doing that. The fact that I prayed for her was satisfactory enough for me but the fact that I didn't give her the slightest clue that I did even brought greater satisfaction and fulfilment.

Jesus told His followers,

> But you, when you pray, go into your room, and when you have shut your door, pray to your Father who is in the secret place; and your Father who sees in secret will reward you openly.
>
> — MATTHEW 6:6 NKJV

Eugene Peterson reworded that verse to bring out the *"why"*. He writes:

> Here's what I want you to do: Find a quiet, secluded place so you won't be tempted to role-play before God. Just be there as simply and honestly as you can manage. The focus will shift from you to God, and you will begin to sense his grace.

So today, take some time to specifically pray secretly for someone. Yours is just to pray; leave the

Secret Prayers | 103

rest to God.

As you do so, may the Lord answer even your own unvoiced prayers as well.

Amen.

Over to you . . .

- *As said in the post, today's challenge is simple: Take some time to specifically pray secretly for someone. (Yours is just to pray; leave the rest to God.)*

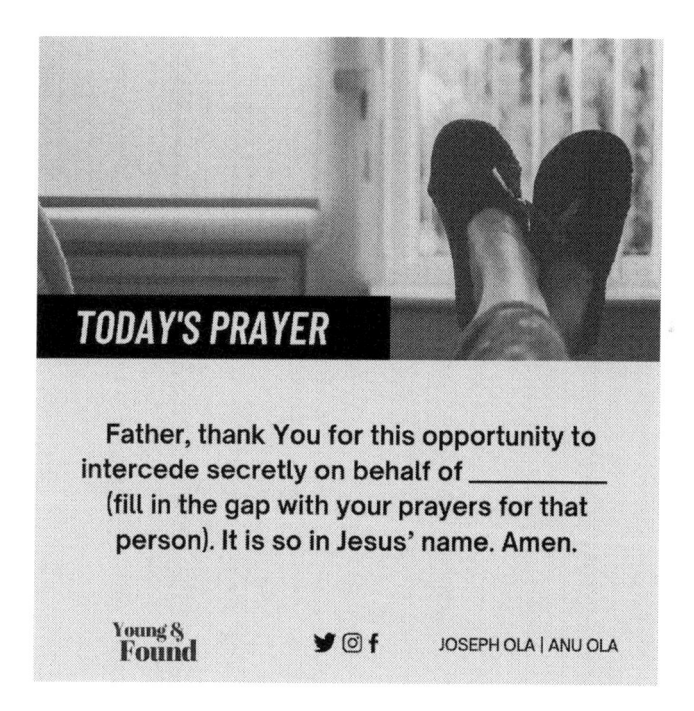

TODAY'S PRAYER

Father, thank You for this opportunity to intercede secretly on behalf of _____ (fill in the gap with your prayers for that person). It is so in Jesus' name. Amen.

Young & Found   JOSEPH OLA | ANU OLA

27

KILL YOUR HATE
BY ANU OLA

The cravings of the self-life are obvious: Sexual immorality, lustful thoughts, pornography, 20 chasing after things instead of God, manipulating others, hatred of those who get in your way...
(Galatians 5:19-20 TPT)

You can only hate from afar. Once you get to know the cause or the person, hate dissipates. Understanding dawns. Acceptance follows. The thing about hatred is that it thrives in the darkness of our ignorance. Hate is clingy. It needs the substance of our point of view—which is never the full picture. You can pick up a novel and dive into a chapter in the middle and conclude that you hate the story, but without knowing the beginning and the end of it, how justifiable is your conclusion?

Rather than letting hatred thrive on the soil of your heart—which only sees in part—always remember that the choice is yours. God owns you—but He made You as a choosing being (like Himself!). You get to choose how to respond in any given situation. No matter how noble the cause is, before you start getting ahead of yourself, read the lines. Then read it again. No haste. Is the cause all that has been said it is? Are you sure? Is he really who you have heard him to be? Does she mirror the description you've been given? Place evidence over knowledge. Be there. Be it. Review the cause. Explore the options—the *how*, the *what*, the *whys*, the *what-ifs*, and the *maybes*. Then make your conclusions.

Can the effect be treated with some other output? Can YOU accept? Can YOU live with them or it? Is it acceptable? Are they acceptable? Can YOU ignore them or it? Can YOU live blissfully without tweaking the cause? Do YOU understand 'the what'? Can YOU let it die lonely?

To become hateful is easy. But with a bit of perspective and a permission for love to control your life, it can be killed.

Kill Your Hate | 107

Over to you . . .

- *How will you complete this statement: "I hate _____."*
- *What's in that blank for you? Check with the tips given in today's episode if your conclusion is justifiable under God. Then take appropriate action.*

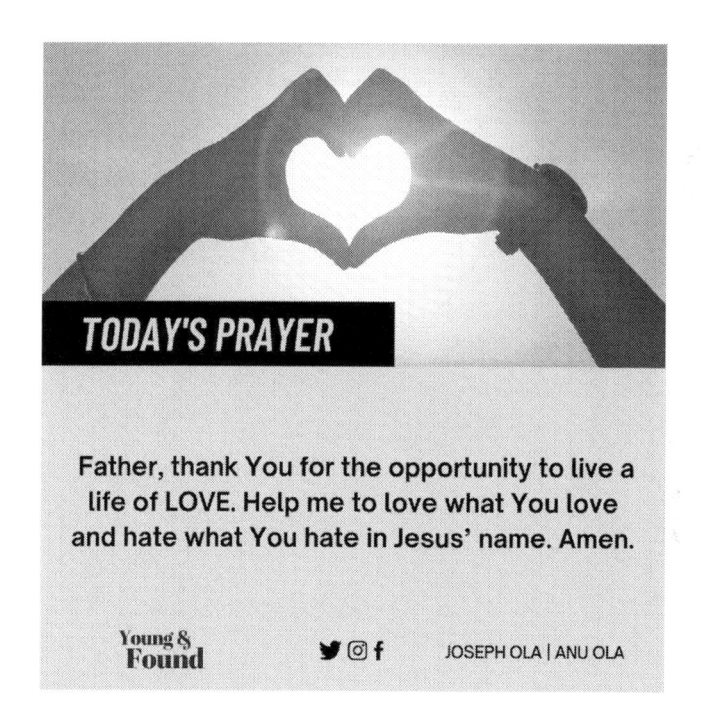

TODAY'S PRAYER

Father, thank You for the opportunity to live a life of LOVE. Help me to love what You love and hate what You hate in Jesus' name. Amen.

Young & Found

JOSEPH OLA | ANU OLA

THE OTHER SIDE OF WISDOM
BY JOSEPH OLA

*"If you cover up your sin you'll never do well. But if you
confess your sins and forsake them,
you will be kissed by mercy."
(Proverbs 28:13 TPT)*

The day started with one of those normal conversations that somehow turned south between my then fiancée and I. One moment, I was happy to be hearing the voice on the other end of the line, the next moment, I felt like hanging up on her and typing out a four-word text to send to her:

It's over between us!

(I dare say that if a supposed marriage-intended relationship hadn't come to that point, both parties may be deceiving themselves).

In this particular instance though, I was clearly in the wrong. Clearly. I managed to get the conversation to a close, then spent the rest of my journey to college reasoning out what I should do amidst tears. Few minutes later, I knew just the right thing to do. At the impulse of wisdom—the other side of wisdom—I picked up my phone and typed a message of apology. I took responsibility for my mistake and appreciated Eleos for bringing it up. She replied later and we eventually got back on the same page. (We got back so much that I married her three months later...LOL)

The bible says it's wisdom to "overlook an offence." Absolutely. But I think there's another side of wisdom which prompts us to both acknowledge and take responsibility for our offence.

> Prudence makes one slow to anger and his glory is to overlook an offence...When someone wrongs you, it is a great virtue to ignore it.
>
> — Proverbs 19:11 TLV, GNT

That's wisdom! But Proverbs 28:13 TLB also reminds us:

> A man who refuses to admit his mistakes can never be successful. But if he confesses and forsakes them, he gets another chance.

That's the other side of wisdom.

Ask for both.

Over to you . . .

- *Is there a mistake you need to own and take responsibility for today?*
- *What are you waiting for? DO IT. (Tip: Apologise. Restitute. Make the phone call. Type the message. Buy the gift. Do whatever you need to do that communicates that you are truly sorry and acknowledge your fault.)*

TODAY'S PRAYER

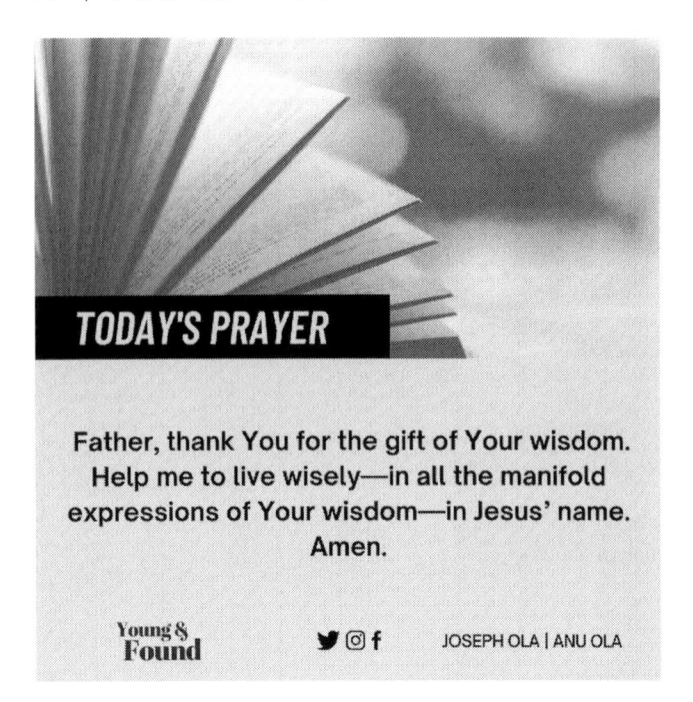

Father, thank You for the gift of Your wisdom. Help me to live wisely—in all the manifold expressions of Your wisdom—in Jesus' name. Amen.

JOSEPH OLA | ANU OLA

29

LOOKING FOR SOME MAGIC?
BY JOSEPH OLA

"Keep vigilant watch over your heart;
that's where life starts."
(Proverbs 4:23 MSG)

The other day, I saw a rather absurd post on Facebook. It was the picture of two trains almost colliding at an intersection. The picture had this caption:

1. Open This Pic.
2. Click On Like
3. Comment 88 and See The Magic!

In 2 days of uploading the picture, it had been shared by 1,000 people and had generated 80,000 comments. Looking at the comment section, however, shortly after someone's "88" comment, you are very likely to find another comment from the same person saying

> "As for me, I didn't see any magic..."

Makes me wonder... Why are so many people drawn to deception? Why do some people tend to enjoy the thrill of deception, and by so doing, deaden their receptivity to the genuine? Many are struggling with negative addictions because they are drawn by the power of the deception of their chains. Worse still, many are crossing the thin line between entertainment and occultism without even knowing it—just following the sway of the attractiveness of their deception. The devil keeps making darkness a creatively and distractingly inviting phenomenon. Don't be caught in its field.

How? By going for and holding on to the truth! Yes, magic can be entertaining, but you hardly can tell which is innocent and which is occult. You don't want to open up your spirit to unnecessary torment cloaked in some deceptive and harmless entertainment. Guard your eyes and ears jealously—they are the gateways to your heart (see Pro. 4:23).[1]

> You will know the truth, and the truth will set you free.
>
> — JOHN 8:32 CEV

Who needs some magic when you've got a living miracle on your inside?

Over to you . . .

- *Tweet or post that last statement on social media today: "Who needs some magic when you've got a living miracle on your inside?" #YoungAndFound*

TODAY'S PRAYER

Father, thank You for the miracle resident in me. Saturate my life with Your truth that I may be free indeed in Jesus' name.
Amen.

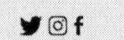

GODLY MONEY MANAGEMENT (1)
BY JOSEPH OLA

*"...You cannot serve God and
the power of money at the same time."*
(Matthew 6:24 PHILLIPS)

Over the next couple of days, we will look at few principles to have at the back of our minds with regards to how we are to handle money as believers. The conversion experience of our heart and mind should translate to a change in how we view and handle money.

1. God owns it all—everything we have

As much as the world tells us that all we earn is ours to do as we please with, we understand as believers that God is the One Who gives us the ability and capacity to earn anything. It is God Who enables us to produce wealth through our work, skills and gifts. He warned the Israelites,

> When you become successful, don't say, "I'm rich, and I've earned it all myself." Instead, remember that the Lord your God gives you the strength to make a living.
>
> — Deuteronomy 8:17-18 CEV

2. Money readily contests for the place of 'God' in our lives

In the Sermon on the Mount, Jesus said,

> How could you worship two gods at the same time? You will have to hate one and love the other, or be devoted to one and despise the other. You can't worship the true God while enslaved to the god of money!
>
> — Matthew 6:24 TPT

Here, Jesus refers to money as a *master* we serve at the expense of serving God—and, of course, that would be violating the very first commandment to have no other gods besides the only true God.

The devil wants the love of money to take first place in your life other than your Creator God. Don't let him.

Over to you . . .

- *Ask God to show you how you can apply these principles to your financial life.*

TODAY'S PRAYER

Father, thank You because all that I have is from You. Help me to acknowledge this practically in how I manage my finance in Jesus' name.
Amen.

JOSEPH OLA | ANU OLA

31

GODLY MONEY MANAGEMENT (2)
BY JOSEPH OLA

"For the love of money is the first step toward all kinds of sin..."
(1 Timothy 6:10 TLB)

3. Love of Money is the root of all evil

I used to misquote our text verse today as "money is the root of all evil." This is clearly false. It is the *love* of money, not money itself, that leads to different kinds of trouble and evil. Wealth is amoral; in and of itself, it is neither wrong nor right. However, when we allow money to begin to control us, that's when trouble starts.

Earlier in the passage, Paul warns Timothy about false teachers who think that *"the Good News is just a means of making money." (v. 5)* In pointing Timothy in the direction of the real source of "great gain", Paul names two elements: godliness and contentment (v. 6 NKJV).

To be content, Paul explains further, is to recognise that

> We didn't bring anything into this world, and we won't take anything with us when we leave
>
> — 1 Timothy 6:7 CEV

Everything we have is a gift from God's hands.

Those who have the "love of money" are the ones who are led into temptation and fall into a snare (v. 9) because the love of money leads to all sorts of sin and evil (v. 10).

All that to say this: **The love of money deceives!** Explaining the parable of the sower to the disciples, Jesus said

> the seduction of wealth ... crowd out and choke the Word so that it produces nothing.
>
> — Mark 4:19 TPT

That's what the devil desires for us and he tricks us into that trap by making us crave for more and more money. The more we go after money, the less we sense a 'need' for God because this lure of money promises to give us all that God gives. Don't fall for it.

Over to you . . .

- *Have you ever found yourself choosing what will be more financial gratifying over what will spiritually edify? Ask God for mercy.*

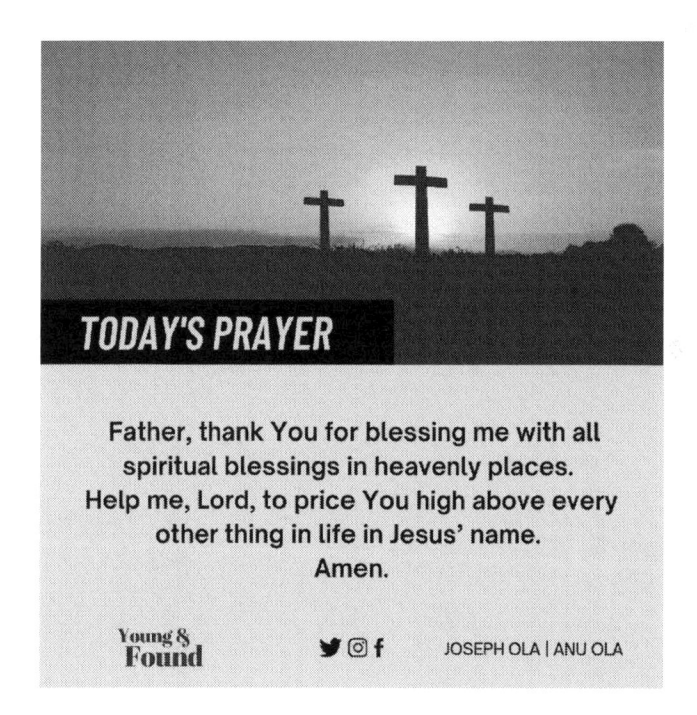

TODAY'S PRAYER

Father, thank You for blessing me with all spiritual blessings in heavenly places.
Help me, Lord, to price You high above every other thing in life in Jesus' name.
Amen.

JOSEPH OLA | ANU OLA

GODLY MONEY MANAGEMENT (3)
BY JOSEPH OLA

"Remind the wealthy to be rich in good works of extravagant generosity, willing to share with others."
(1 Timothy 6:18 TPT)

4. Money should serve you

In God's plan, money should be our servant, not the other way round. We are to live with the understanding that the money we have is for God's use in any way He desires for us to use it. When we handle money like this— when money becomes a servant in our hands, the benefits are tremendous!

a. It blesses US.

it is very good if a man has received wealth from the Lord and the good health to enjoy it. To enjoy your work and to accept your lot in life—that is indeed a gift from God. The person who does that will not need to look back with sorrow on his past, for God gives him joy.

— Ecclesiastes 5:19 TLB

b. It blesses OTHERS.

Give generously and generous gifts will be given back to you, shaken down to make room for more. Abundant gifts will pour out upon you with such an overflowing measure that it will run over the top! Your measurement of generosity becomes the measurement of your return.

— Luke 6:38 TPT

c. We gain "TRUE LIFE"

Tell those rich in this world's wealth to quit being so full of themselves and so obsessed with money, which is here today and gone tomorrow. Tell them to go after God, who piles on all the riches we could ever manage—to do good, to be rich in helping others, to be extravagantly generous. If they do that, they'll build a treasury that will last, gaining life that is truly life.

— 1 Timothy 6:17-19 MSG

May these blessings become our experience. Amen.

Over to you . . .

- *Think of someone you can be a blessing to financially right now and send them a financial gift. (Tip: It doesn't have to be a huge amount.)*

TODAY'S PRAYER

Father, thank You for making me a blessing. Help me to always leverage on my financial prosperity to be a blessing to others and contribute to advancing Your kingdom in Jesus' name.
Amen.

JOSEPH OLA | ANU OLA

GODLY MONEY MANAGEMENT (4)
BY JOSEPH OLA

"For the love of money is the first step toward all kinds of sin..."
(1 Timothy 6:10 TLB)

5. The 'God first' Principle

In wrapping up our series on Godly Money Management, we need to also mention the 'God-first' principle. God established a principle in the Bible called the **first fruit principle** whereby God lays rightful claim on the first portion (be it of animals, harvest or humans). Likewise, making our relationship with God the first and the best part of our lives must find expression in how we manage our income. *Tithing* is a numerical expression of this much bigger principle in the Old Testament.

While the New Testament nowhere prescribes that Christians should submit to a legalistic tithe system nor designates a certain percentage of income a person should set aside, it does mention that what we give (financially) in church should depend "on how much the Lord has helped you earn." (1 Corinthians 16:2 TLB).

What does that look like? Bearing in mind the countless references on the benefits of giving in the New Testament, it makes sense that we are to give as much as we are able. Sometimes that means giving more than 10 percent; sometimes that may mean giving less. In any case, the God-first principle will stir up the desire in us to want to go above-and-beyond in our contributions to the advancement of God's mission on the earth.

I have found, however, that if we don't train ourselves as young people in the discipline of generously honouring God with our substance, the more we earn, the less likely it is that we will give in proportion to how much the Lord has helped us earn. In any case,

> Each man should give what he has decided in his heart to give, not reluctantly or under compulsion, for God loves a cheerful giver

— 2 Corinthians 9:7 NIV

Over to you . . .

- *Whether you tithe or not, ensure you are contributing generously and regularly to the cause of God in your local church and beyond.*

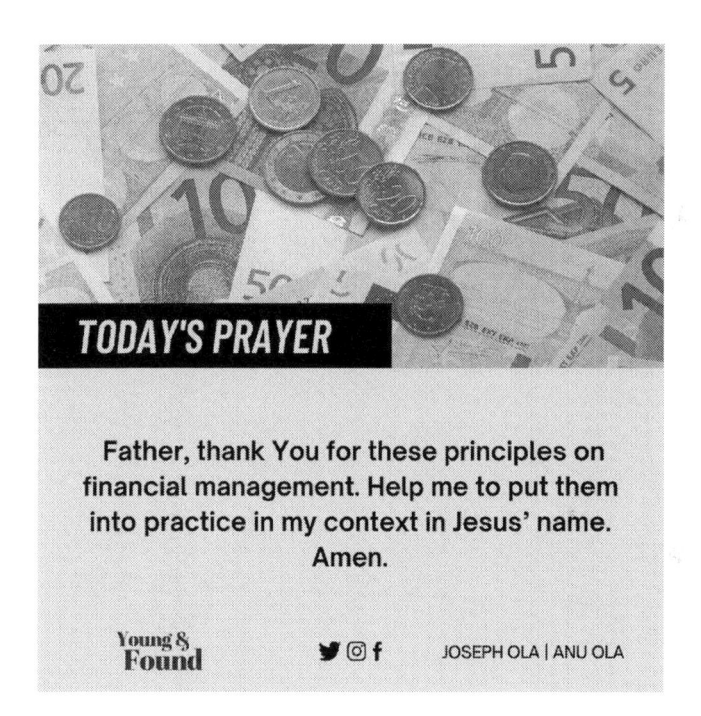

TODAY'S PRAYER

Father, thank You for these principles on financial management. Help me to put them into practice in my context in Jesus' name. Amen.

Young & Found

JOSEPH OLA | ANU OLA

HOW TO JOURNEY INTO THE UNKNOWN (1)
BY JOSEPH OLA

"Whatever He says to you, do it."
(John 2:5 AMP)

On the 30th of April, 2012, I embarked on a journey that would shape the rest of my life. I was a fresh graduate of Microbiology. I have had quite a number of job offers that I had turned down. And I had an interview scheduled for that date to take up a teaching role. However, I left all of that to head to Lagos, Nigeria in pursuance of a persuasion I felt in my heart that God was calling me into pastoral ministry. It was plainly a journey into the unknown.

Looking back in retrospect eight years later, I couldn't be more glad that I yielded to that prompting. It will take a whole book to let you into the details, but the summary of it is that God has been faithful.

In reality, we all get to such junctions in life when we have to take a first step into the unknown. How do we navigate that? I thought to share here three lessons that helped me in my journey into the unknown.

1. Trust God's voice more than facts

We always have the choice to go by the message the Spirit of God is communicating with us per time, or to go by the facts available—and more often than none, the two will conflict. We need to get to that point where we develop a resolution to prioritise God's Word above all else.

At the wedding where Jesus performed His first miracle at the plea of his mum, Mary made it a point of duty to leave this all-important instruction with the servers:

> "Whatever Jesus tells you, make sure that you do it!"

— John 2:5 TPT

So when Jesus said

> "Now take some water and give it to the man in charge of the feast." **The servants did as Jesus told them.**

— Verse 8 CEV

The result? A miracle! Indeed, factually, it was water, but the virtue of obedience often paves way for the miraculous. Receive the grace to obey. Amen.

Over to you . . .

- *Is there something God has been laying in your heart to do? Take the first step today!*

TODAY'S PRAYER

Father, thank You for being the Architect of my life. Give me the grace to yield to Your promptings and obey Your instructions in Jesus' name.
Amen.

Young & Found   🐦 📷 f   JOSEPH OLA | ANU OLA

HOW TO JOURNEY INTO THE UNKNOWN (2)
BY JOSEPH OLA

*"Where there is no [wise, intelligent] guidance, the people fall [and go off course like a ship without a helm], But **in the abundance of [wise and godly] counselors there is victory.**"*
(Proverbs 11:14 AMP)

2. Surround yourself with wise counsel

After I started sensing the promptings to pursue pastoral ministry in April 2012, one of the succours I enjoyed was the gift of godly relationships. When I shared what I felt the Lord was leading me into with a few of my destiny friends and with my mentor, what I received was an overwhelming outpouring of confirmations, counsel and prayers.

I never realised the true worth of godly friendships until that point in my life. My parents waited on God with me for more clarity. My friends gave prophetic messages that are still being fulfilled till date. My mentor heartily prayed for me after confirming what I received in my heart.

There is a lot of wisdom in Solomon's recommendation:

> Without consultation *and* wise advice, plans are frustrated, But with many counselors they are established and succeed.
>
> — Proverbs 15:22 AMP

He said it again and again in hopes that we'll get it. (See Proverbs 11:14[1] and 24:6[2]). This is why it is very important to build purposeful friendships. If you surround yourself with those who are going nowhere, their counsel will reflect their purposelessness, and it can be contagious. Paul says it this way:

> Don't fool yourselves. Bad friends will destroy you.
>
> ...If you listen to them you will start acting like them.

— 1 Corinthians 15:33 CEV & TLB

What kind of friends are in your inner circle right now? Are they the kind that can inspire you into the pursuit of your purpose?

Over to you . . .

- *Do you have 'destiny friends' — people who resonate with what God is up to in your life and who can speak freely to you and/or confront you when you are getting it wrong?*
- *If you do, thank God for them. If you don't, ask God for them.*

TODAY'S PRAYER

Father, thank You for the gift of counsel. Lord, order my steps in Your will and always instruct me in the way that I should go—and help me to obey in Jesus' name.
Amen.

JOSEPH OLA | ANU OLA

HOW TO JOURNEY INTO THE UNKNOWN (3)
BY JOSEPH OLA

They are fooled by the desire to get rich and to have all kinds of other things ... and they never produce anything.
(Mark 4:19 CEV)

3. Go for fulfilment; not money

As I mentioned two days ago, I had other options prior to this pursuit. Between February and April, I had been offered a job at a bank, in a government owned resource centre, and I had a teaching role on the queue. Monetarily, all those other options were more promising, but I found that I made the right call in prioritising fulfilment over money.

It is faulty thinking to reason that what God is calling you to do—or what you feel passionate about—won't bring you profit. It is such reasoning that makes people postpone the *discovery* and *pursuit* of their calling (and the discovery is as important as the pursuit).

In fact, taking money out of the equation has helped many people discover what they are here for. They asked themselves,

> *If money was not going to be a limitation:*
> *What would I create?*
> *Who would I help?*
> *What would I contribute?*
> *What would an ideal day look like for me?*

What I have realised over the years is that when you discover your calling, it is like finding the task for which the Creator created you, and He never sends anyone on a *mission* without making adequate *provision* to see the mission accomplished. Eventually, your calling will attract dividends. Sometimes, it will be monetary, other times it will be in forms weightier than money. In either case, you are fulfilled. Nothing beats that.

So my question to you today is this: *What would you do, if you could, for free?*

Over to you...

- *Answer that question honestly — "What would you do, if you could, for free?"*
- *You can share this insightful question with someone in your world that needs it, too.*

TODAY'S PRAYER

Father, thank You for the gift of life. Help me to live in pursuit of fulfilment and not money in Jesus' name.
Amen.

Young & Found | JOSEPH OLA | ANU OLA

TELL IT!
BY ANU OLA

All praise to the God and Father of our Master, Jesus the Messiah! Father of all mercy! God of all healing counsel! He comes alongside us when we go through hard times, and before you know it, he brings us alongside someone else who is going through hard times so that we can be there for that person just as God was there for us.
(2 Corinthians 1:3-4 MSG)

Our stories bring us closer. Our stories stop suicidal thoughts. Our stories increase confidence. Our stories bridge gaps. Our stories reduce racism and form bonds that race can't cut through. And our stories hold no preference because life happens to all of us.

How will Bukky know that it is okay to still bed wet at 26 unless Anu shares how she got through hers? How will Esther know it is okay to have sexual cravings for married men unless Peter shares how his wife got through hers? How will the world be a better place for others unless we make it so?

So, let grace happen here. Share your shame. Share your pain. Tell it! Don't handle it alone otherwise it will break you. Share your joys, your struggles, your disappointments—share them. With each sharing comes enlightenment. Then freedom.

Does lie come easily for you and you're being mocked for it? Is yours lust? Is it gossip? Is it gambling? Is it deep resentment for other's success? Is it hate? Or your mom? Your dad? We all struggle with things. We are all going through restoration.

Paul was like us. In spite of being a prominent lawyer, Jesus lover, prolific writer, and God's wingman . . . in spite of his unrivalled access to revelations and visions, he confessed he had struggles. I think we are in good company!

Over to you . . .

- *Sharing intimate details about parts of our lives for which we are not so proud will definitely be difficult, but when we put it in the perspective of helping others break free and grow into their best selves, we find the motivation to share unreservedly.*
- *If you are struggling to do this, ask God for help.*

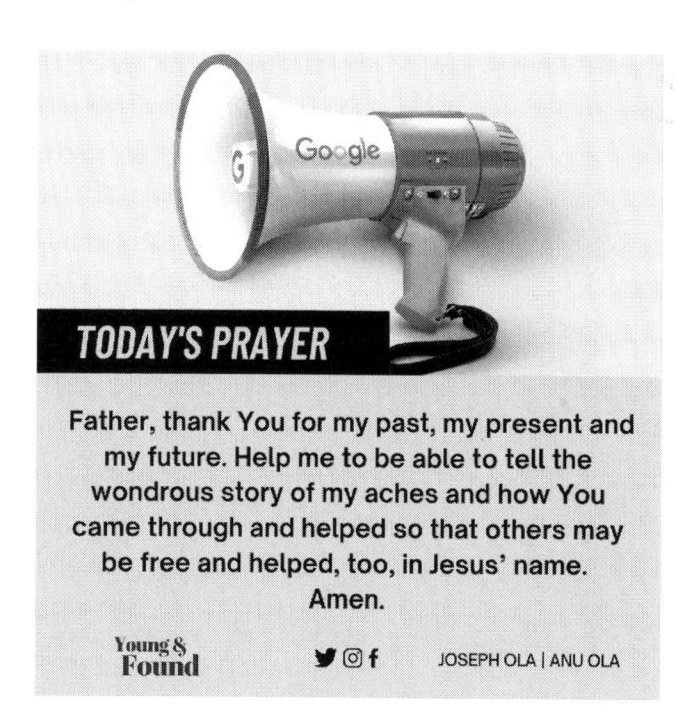

TODAY'S PRAYER

Father, thank You for my past, my present and my future. Help me to be able to tell the wondrous story of my aches and how You came through and helped so that others may be free and helped, too, in Jesus' name.
Amen.

Young & Found   🐦 📷 f   JOSEPH OLA | ANU OLA

LASTMINUTE.COM (1)
BY JOSEPH OLA

Teach us to number our days and recognize how few they are; help us to spend them as we should. (Psalm 90:12 TLB)

I don't know about you, but I've always been a *last minute* guy. All through my Bible College programme and my first Masters degree, I could count on my finger tips how many times I submitted an essay earlier than the due date. I always submitted *on* the due date. I think we can use with some time management principles from God's Word.

1. Acknowledge God in your day-to-day living.

That sounds simple, but the fact is that how we will manage our time depends largely on both *what* is important to us and *who* is important to us. If you acknowledge God—the creator of time—in your time management by spending quality time with Him daily, chances are He will give you the wisdom to live wisely through each day. Some find it most rewarding to do this first thing in the morning. Others prefer when other family members have gone to bed. Whichever works for you, ensure you are spending time with the Time Giver.

Ephesians 2:10 tells us in so many words that God intends for us to "spend our lives doing the good things he had already planned for us to do." (ERV). So there is wisdom in asking the Lord each morning to help us identify the good things that He has planned for us to do on that particular day. Ask the Lord to show you *how* and *when* and *to whom* you might minister by using the good gifts and talents that He has given you. We can also ask the Lord to help us manage our recreational time, our opportunities to evangelise and our family time so that our relationships are made strong and joyful.

2. Take Responsibility for how you manage your time.

We need to take seriously Paul's admonition to redeem the time—to make the most of the time God has given us (Ephesians 5:16). We have a choice to make in this regard. If you don't manage your time, somebody else will manage it for you.

We will consider few more tips tomorrow.

Over to you . . .

- *How would you rate your time management skills?*
- *Start inculcating the habit of spending time with God daily, asking Him to show You how best to spend each day in primary pursuit of the things He had planned for you to do daily.*

TODAY'S PRAYER

Father, it's refreshing to know that You have my time in Your hands. Help me identify the good things that You have planned for me to do in Jesus' name.
Amen.

Young & Found

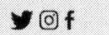

JOSEPH OLA | ANU OLA

LASTMINUTE.COM (2)
BY JOSEPH OLA

*... be sure that everything is done properly
in a good and orderly way.
(1 Corinthians 14:40 TLB)*

3. Make Plans and Be Organised.

We can have all the goals and dreams that we desire, but until we put those into the context of deadlines, how can we advance towards fulfilment? Sometimes, I have so many things that I know I ought to do jammed up in my head. But thank God for tools and apps that do make scheduling and being organised more realistic. Use these tools to stay organised as you work, thus honouring God's counsel to us to do things orderly (Exodus 40:1-16; 1 Corinthians 14:40). Of course, what being organised and orderly looks like will differ for each of us.

Making plans will help you prioritise. If you devote your most productive hours of the day—be it in the morning, noon or (mid)night—to the tasks that are directly related to your goals, you achieve more on the long run.

4. Reflect on each day and Journal.

Some do this at the end of each day, others at the beginning of the next day, but the principle is very useful. I didn't know my life is such a bundle of lessons until I started doing this. I will reflect on the previous day at the beginning of a new day, make a note of any lesson I had learnt, unlearnt or relearnt, and make a prayer from emerging themes.

In evaluating your day, you can follow that pattern, too. You can go further to compare what you did with what you intended to do and ask yourself honest questions about how you managed time. Thank God for your wins. Learn from your losses, and repeat the cycle all over again.

We will consider one more tip tomorrow.

Over to you . . .

- *If you have been journalling before, spend some time reading your previous entries in your journal and thank God for the lessons you have learnt and the prayers that had been answered.*
- *If you are yet to start journalling, however, buy a journal to use for that purpose today or open an electronic file/mobile app that can help you do this.*

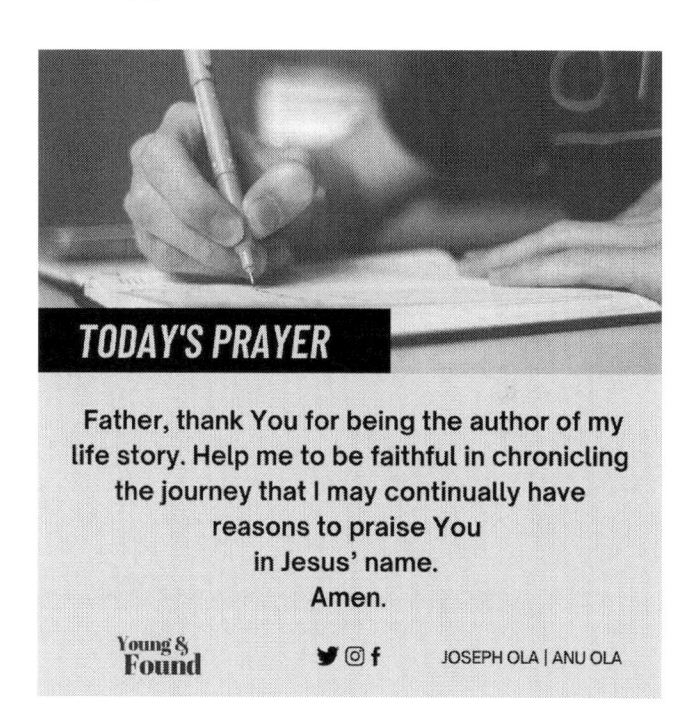

TODAY'S PRAYER

Father, thank You for being the author of my life story. Help me to be faithful in chronicling the journey that I may continually have reasons to praise You
in Jesus' name.
Amen.

Young & Found

JOSEPH OLA | ANU OLA

LASTMINUTE.COM (3)
BY JOSEPH OLA

Teach us to number our days and recognize how few they are; help us to spend them as we should. (Psalm 90:12 TLB)

5. Eliminate unnecessary tasks on your to-do list.

In his book *Success Gods Way,* Charles Stanley writes:

> Charles Schwab, the president of Bethlehem Steel, hired a consultant and said to him. "If you'll show me how I and other top managers in our company can use our time better, I will pay you a fee of whatever you ask within reason."

The man said, "All right." He then gave Schwab a blank sheet of paper and said, "I want you to write on this sheet of paper all the important things you need to do tomorrow and list them in order of their priority. As number one, put the most important thing you should do tomorrow. As number two, put the second most important thing you should do, and so forth. Then when you go into work tomorrow morning, start with the first thing on your list and stick with it until you finish it. Then move on to number two, and so forth. You more than likely will not be able to accomplish all the things on your list in a given day, but you will have accomplished the most important thing on your list or at least made a major effort regarding it. Then tomorrow night, make a new list for the upcoming day. Do this for several weeks and let me know what happens."

I apply the same principle these days and it has been revolutionary. I use an app called Todoist to do this. I have some recurrent weekly or monthly responsibilities that are programmed in and tagged with a priority level. I incorporate other schedules as the need arises. So at a glance I can see what I've got to do each day and in order of priority. You can give this a try, too.

My wife is also fond of scheduling any upcoming event or task on our shared Google Calendar. That way, we are in sync regarding what needs to be done (especially in the home front).

Having said all these, however, we will still fail every now and again in managing our times wisely. The goal is to be faithful, not perfect. And never forget where we started from: Acknowledging God. We can talk to Him about all of these tips and how to apply them in our individual contexts.

May you become a better time manager in Jesus' name.

Over to you . . .

- *If you already have tools that help you stay on top of your schedules and responsibilities, that's great. Share the resources you use with others who may benefit from them.*
- *If you don't, take a moment to research into tips and tools that can be applicable in your context and matching your preferences. You can start here.*[1]

TODAY'S PRAYER

Father, thank You for the daily gift of 24 hours. Help me to always utilise these each day in a way that maximally gives You the glory in Jesus' name.
Amen.

JOSEPH OLA | ANU OLA

NOTES

Preface

1. Knapton, Sarah, "Young People Are 'Lost Generation' Who Can No Longer Fix Gadgets, Warns Professor." *The Telegraph*, December 28, 2014, https://www.telegraph.co.uk/news/science/science-news/11298927/Young-people-are-lost-generation-who-can-no-longer-fix-gadgets-warns-professor.html.
2. Göke, Niklas, "Dear Millennials — a Letter to the Lost Generation." *Medium*, March 10, 2017, https://medium.com/better-humans/dear-millennials-a-letter-to-the-lost-generation-bd3b60964ed8.
3. Voas, David, "A Lost Generation." *Church Times*, January 12, 2018, https://www.churchtimes.co.uk/articles/2018/12-january/features/features/a-lost-generation.
4. Lowrey, Annie, "Millennials Are the New Lost Generation." *The Atlantic*, April 13, 2020, https://www.theatlantic.com/ideas/archive/2020/04/millennials-are-new-lost-generation/609832/.
5. Khazan, Olga, "The Millennial Mental-Health Crisis." *The Atlantic*, June 11, 2020, https://www.theatlantic.com/health/archive/2020/06/why-suicide-rates-among-millennials-are-rising/612943/.
6. Pew Research Center, "The Age Gap in Religion Around the World," The Age Gap in Religion Around the World, 2018, http://www.pewforum.org/2018/06/13/the-age-gap-in-religion-around-the-world/.
7. Pew Research Center.
8. Barna Group, 'Key Findings', *The Connected Generation:* , 2019 <https://theconnectedgeneration.com/key-findings/> [accessed 29 September 2020].

6. Time-Out

1. **Exodus 20:8-11 New International Version (NIV)** — "Remember the Sabbath day by keeping it holy. **9** Six days you shall labor and do all your work, **10** but the seventh day is a sabbath to the Lord your God. On it you shall not do any work, neither you, nor your son or daughter, nor your male or female servant, nor your animals, nor any foreigner residing in your towns. **11** For in six days the Lord made the heavens and the earth, the sea, and all that is in them, but he rested on the seventh day. Therefore the Lord blessed the Sabbath day and made it holy.

11. #NOSUM

1. **1 John 1:9 The Passion Translation (TPT)** — But if we freely admit our sins *when his light uncovers them*, he will be faithful to forgive us every time. God is just to forgive us our sins *because of Christ*, and he will continue to cleanse us from all unrighteousness.

20. There's an "Angel" in You!

1. **Matthew 5:16 Living Bible (TLB)** — Don't hide your light! Let it shine for all; let your good deeds glow for all to see, so that they will praise your heavenly Father.

29. Looking for Some Magic?

1. **Proverbs 4:23 The Passion Translation (TPT)** —
    So above all, guard the affections of your heart,
    for they affect all that you are.
    Pay attention to the welfare of your innermost being,
    for from there flows the wellspring of life.

35. How To Journey Into the Unknown (2)

1. **Proverbs 11:14 The Message (MSG)** — Without good direction, people lose their way; the more wise counsel you follow, the better your chances.
2. **Proverbs 24:6 Living Bible (TLB)** — Don't go to war without wise guidance; there is safety in many counselors.

40. lastminute.com (3)

1. Claybury International, "A Time for Everything – 10 Time Management Tips for Christian Leaders." *Claybury International*, September 10, 2020, http://christian-leadership.org/a-time-for-everything-10-time-management-tips-for-christian-leaders-2/.

INDEX

Addictions — Days 10, 11, 23, 24, 29
Attitude — Days 4, 13, 17, 20, 27
Bible Study — Day 5
Competence — Day 1
Faith — Days 14, 15, 34, 35, 36
Fear — Days 14, 15
Fun — Days 6, 18
Hearing God's voice — Days 3, 34
Honesty — Days 1, 13, 16, 26, 37, 39
Honour — Days 2, 12, 21, 33, 39
Integrity — Days 1, 16, 37
Leadership — Days 1, 22, 34, 35, 36
Life lessons — Days 2, 12, 19, 20, 25, 27, 28, 29, 37
Love — Days 4, 9, 12, 16, 17, 19, 21, 22, 25, 27, 30, 31, 33
Marriage — Days 8, 9, 11, 13, 17, 22, 28
Masturbation — Day 8, 10, 23
Money — Days 30, 31, 32, 33
Parents — Day 12
Pioneering — Days 34, 35, 36
Pornography — Days 10, 11, 27
Prayer — Days 3, 5, 26, 35, 39

Premarital sex — Days 8, 9
Purpose — Days 7, 20, 34, 35, 36, 38, 39, 40
Rest — Day 6
Sex — Days 8, 9, 10, 11
Struggles — Days 3, 9, 23, 24, 29, 37
Submission — Days 7, 17, 22
Time management — Days 38, 39, 40
Wisdom — Days 2, 13, 19, 20, 25, 27, 28, 29, 35, 37, 38

ABOUT THE AUTHORS

Joseph ministers at The Apostolic Church, Liverpool UK. He's the author of a few books including *Waiting Compass: Finding God when He seems to delay*; *Is This Opportunity From God?: 7 Checkpoints for Discerning Divine Opportunities*; *#Unaddicted: Finding Freedom from Sex-related Addictions* and more recently, *Pandemic Joy: Making Sense of Life's Uncertainties.* Anu is a law graduate and works in a law firm. She is involved in Children and Youth ministry. She is outdoorsy and blogs at eleosblisshouse.org. They co-authored *Marriage in View* and co-host **Alive Mentorship Group**, an online mentorship platform reaching thousands of young adults. They live in Liverpool, UK with their two sons, Joshua OdodoOluwa and Samuel OkikiOluwa.

- facebook.com/josephkolawole
- twitter.com/iamjosephola
- instagram.com/josephkolawole
- youtube.com/OlaJosephKolawole
- linkedin.com/in/josephkolawole

ABOUT THE BOOK

It is unfortunate that today's young adults and teens have been labeled 'a lost generation'. To be *young*, in the eyes of popular media, is to be *lost*. But this does not have to be the case. Reflecting on their life experiences and the honest questions they have been asked by teenagers and young adults, Joseph and Anu share practical and biblical wisdom on the complex everyday challenges that young Christians face. Subjects covered include *personal development, hearing God's voice, sex and sexuality, parent-youth relationships, faith, integrity, fun, marriage, managing weaknesses, prayer, pioneering, time and money management* — to mention but a few. Each day's reflection is accompanied with practical tips on applying the message and a prayer. These reflections have already helped thousands of millennials realise that they are young but not lost; they are *young and found* in Christ. It is the authors' prayer that this becomes the testimony of everyone who reads this.

Waiting Compass: Finding God when He seems to delay

Waiting Compass: Finding God when He seems to delay

WHERE IS THE ALL-POWERFUL GOD?

If God is so loving and all-powerful, how come He is missing in inaction? How come He's silent to my legitimate requests? He promised that none of His shall be barren. Where is the baby? He promised that the prayer of faith will heal the sick. Why am I still sick? He promised to answer before I call. Where is the answer after calling and calling again? **WHERE IS GOD?**

It's a question you've probably asked. It's a question Joseph has definitely asked when his reality seemed decades away from what God had promised. Thus, in five 'peaces' of transformational thoughts, Joseph hands us a compass which points us in the direction where God may be found in times like that. With lots of stories from his personal journey, Joseph writes with such simplicity and clarity that drives home the message and leaves the seeker immersed in the unwavering hope of God's reassuring promise: "I will never leave you, nor forsake you."

#Unaddicted: Finding Freedom from Sex-related Addictions

#Unaddicted: Finding Freedom from Sex-related Addictions

In his years of engaging with teenagers and young adults, the question Joseph has been most frequently asked is on **overcoming sexual addictions—especially pornography and masturbation.**

This book brings together in one volume Joseph's liberating thoughts on how to do this, sharing unreservedly from his journey through the same struggles.

The book is easy-to-read and has been a helpful resource for many teenagers and young adults.

∼

Bumpy But Sweet | A Love Story: LESSONS LEARNT ON FINDING A LIFE PARTNER AND BUILDING A GODLY RELATIONSHIP

Bumpy But Sweet | A Love Story: LESSONS LEARNT ON FINDING A LIFE PARTNER AND BUILDING A GODLY RELATIONSHIP

Anu married Joseph on the same day she graduated with a First Class from her LLB degree. Their marriage story went viral on the internet partly for the unique combination of marrying and graduating on a single day and partly because of their incredible love story. This ebook details an up-close-and-personal look into their love story initially shared on an online seminar. They answered lots of questions from young adults about love, dating, courtship, sex, and discerning the will of God besides many other elements that constitute a godly marriage. The book has been a very helpful resource to thousands of singles and young couples.

Is This Opportunity From God?: 7 Checkpoints for Discerning Divine Opportunities

Is This Opportunity From God?: 7 Checkpoints for Discerning Divine Opportunities

The difference between joy and regret sometimes is being able to discern between what is *good* and what is *God*.

We will be faced with many opportunities in life, but how can we tell which of them is not a distraction from God's best plan for us? In this book, reflecting on scripture and personal experience, Joseph lays out 7 checkpoints to help the reader discern if an opportunity is indeed from God or just another distraction from His best plan. In this book you will learn:

- How to avoid regret
- Positive and negative signs to watch out for in making a choice
- Tips on choosing a life partner

And lots more!

Marriage in View: Ready? Sleep. Go!

Marriage in View: Ready? Sleep. Go!

This book will surely save many young adults from unnecessary heartbreak.

Besides coming into a relationship with God, there is hardly any decision that is of more significance and long-lasting implications than the decision on who to marry. With the increasing misrepresentation of marriage through popular culture, young people are desperate for trustworthy models and principles to guide them through the waters of marriage-in-view relationships, hence this book. Joseph and Anu, through their love story, draw young people to engage with the tested and timeless countercultural principles upon which the institution of marriage is established. Written in a warm and conversational style, the book will teach you:

- guidelines on discovering who to marry;
- answers to questions about dating, courtship, sex and weddings; and
- principles for building a Godly marriage.

Pandemic Joy: Making Sense of Life's Uncertainties

Pandemic Joy: Making Sense of Life's Uncertainties

In this book, Joseph Ola tackles the tricky and very immediate subject of making sense of life's uncertainties as Christians. His contribution is steeped in his reading of scripture and theology interwoven with some thoughtfully chosen Yoruba proverbs and practical illustrations from everyday life. At its core, the book reminds us to live wisely as good citizens whilst holding steadfastly to the joy that belongs to those who follow the way of the risen Christ. For readers who sense they are living in anxious times, this book offers practical wisdom shot through with the joy of the gospel. — **Colin Smith | Dean of Mission Education, Church Mission Society, Oxford**

"An excellent read for anyone struggling to make sense of the uncertainties of life." — **Rev Canon Elaine Jones | Vicar, Church of England, UK.**

"They say a book is only as good as the timing it lands in your world and I would say that this is a timely book for many!" — **Rich Martin | Principal, LIFE Church UK College**

"Rarely is a book quite as topical or as encouraging as Joseph Ola's Pandemic Joy." — **John Neate | Vineyard Churches, UK**

Word Alive
Truth. Freedom. Growth

Inspired by what you just read?
Connect with Joseph.

Follow Joseph's teaching ministry, Word Alive, online.
Visit www.JosephKolawole.org to get FREE resources for your spiritual growth and encouragement, including:

Blog Posts
Downloads of video, audio, and printed material
Joseph's podcast
First look at book excerpts
Mobile content.
You will also find an eStore and special offers.

Follow Joseph on Twitter @iamJosephOla
Or at Facebook.com/JosephKolawole

Printed in Great Britain
by Amazon